Pre- and Postnatal care for Both Baby and Mom

A Practical and Step-by-Step Manual on How to Care of Your Baby and Yourself Starting from the Conception Up To the End of Your Baby´s First Year

Harley Carr

© **Copyright 2020 - All rights reserved.**

The content contained within this book may not be reproduced, duplicated or transmitted without direct written permission from the author or the publisher.

Under no circumstances will any blame or legal responsibility be held against the publisher, or author, for any damages, reparation, or monetary loss due to the information contained within this book, either directly or indirectly.

Legal Notice:

This book is copyright protected. It is only for personal use. You cannot amend, distribute, sell, use, quote or paraphrase any part, or the content within this book, without the consent of the author or publisher.

Disclaimer Notice:

Please note the information contained within this document is for educational and entertainment purposes only. All effort has been executed to present accurate, up to date, reliable, complete information. No warranties of any kind are declared or implied. Readers acknowledge that the author is not engaged in the rendering of legal, financial, medical or professional advice. The content within this book has been derived from various sources. Please consult a licensed professional before attempting any techniques outlined in this book.

By reading this document, the reader agrees that under no circumstances is the author responsible for any losses, direct or indirect, that are incurred as a result of the use of the information contained within this document, including, but not limited to, errors, omissions, or inaccuracies.

Giving birth isn't exactly a vacation. Delivery of your baby is a time when you will likely be staying away from home for at least 24 hours to between 2 to 4 days (Caesarian delivery) and sometimes longer.

Do yourself a favor and have your bag packed before the of the 36th week of your pregnancy. In this way, you won't have to give it an extra thought until those contractions start coming full force. Being prepared reduces stress at the time of delivery. In labor just grab your prepared bag and leave for the Hospital.

You've probably read over a bunch of packing lists that seem beyond comprehensive. You don't need to bring everything and the kitchen sink.

Know what to pack in your Pregnancy Hospital Bag with **"My Hospital Bag Checklist"**

Receive a list of the most important items **to pack in your hospital bag for labor**, the practical things you will actually need during your stay in the Hospital.

Get your **"My Hospital Bag Checklist"** in PDF format by clicking the link below:

https://harleycarrparenting.com/pre-and-postnatal-care-for-both-baby-and-mom-book/

or

Print the document and start to pack as early as 36 weeks.

Let´s get started ...

Enjoy and Best Wishes to your pregnancy journey!

Harley Carr

Table Of Contents

Introduction   **11**

Part 1: Prenatal Care   **21**

Chapter 1: Finding the Right Maternity Care Provider and Check-Up Schedule   **27**

- Choose Your Maternity Care Provider   27
- Check-Up Schedule, Test and Scan/Ultrasound   42

Chapter 2: Healthy Options   **55**

- Healthy Eating Habits When You're Eating for Two   55
- Vitamins for You and Your Baby   62
- Common Illnesses During Pregnancy Like Headaches, Fever, etc.   68

Chapter 3: Frequently Asked Questions About Safety During Pregnancy   **73**

- Deli Meat   73
- Pregnancy and Bed Rest   75
- Make-Up Safety: Read the Label   79
- The Effects of Tobacco, Alcohol, and Caffeine   81
- Pregnancy and Vices   83
- Good Pregnancy Workouts for Fitness   85
- Traveling While Pregnant   87

Chapter 4: Pregnancy Fears and Why You Shouldn't Worry   **93**

- Nausea and Morning Sickness   93

Other Common Pregnancy Problems and Their Solutions	98
Working While Pregnant: Know Your Rights	105

Chapter 5: Late Term Pregnancy Comfort and Preparation — 109

- Maternity Jeans and Undergarments — 109
- Methods to Make Sleep More Comfortable — 114
- Preparing for D-Day — 120

Part Two: Postnatal Care — 125

Chapter 6: Taking Care of Yourself — 127

- Recovering From Labor and Childbirth — 127
- Adapting to Your New Lifestyle — 139
- Getting Comfortable With Chaos — 142
- Adjusting to Your Role and Handling New Baby Stress — 143

Chapter 7: Baby's First Days — 147

- Baby's Appearance — 147
- Bonding: Skin-to-Skin Contact — 149
- Weighing and Measuring — 150
- Vitamin K — 151
- Cord Blood Collection and RH Negative — 154
- Feeding and Sleeping — 155
- Apgar Scores — 156
- Your Baby's First Brush With Their Senses — 157
- Urine and Meconium — 158
- Newborn Issues — 158
- Newborn Screening Test — 160

    Newborn Check-Up Expectations   164

Chapter 8: Baby Essentials: Feeding   167

    Breastfeeding Basics   167

    Bottle Feeding   183

    Introducing Solid Food   190

Chapter 9: Baby Essentials: Clothing, Diapers, Bathing, & Skincare   193

    Baby Clothing   193

    Diapers   197

    Bathing and Skin Care   204

    Common Skin Conditions   210

Chapter 10: Care Provider and Childcare   215

    How to Choose Your Baby's Care Provider   215

    Choosing Your Child Care Provider   224

Chapter 11: Check-Up Schedule and Vaccinations   235

    Check-Up Schedule   235

    Questions and Concerns About Check-Ups   245

    Vaccination Schedule   248

Chapter 12: Baby's Safety and Medical Emergency Concerns   257

    Home and Outdoor Safety   257

    Unwell Baby: When to Seek Help   269

    When to Seek Emergency Care   271

    Traveling With an Infant   274

Conclusion   277

References 283

Introduction

If you're looking at this book, it means you're either pregnant, planning to become pregnant, or you know someone who needs some help with their pregnancy. Either way, congratulations are in order. Having a baby is a remarkable, unforgettable, and euphoric experience like no other, though it's filled with many ups and downs. The first time a couple sits down to have the baby chat is the very moment when you feel closest to each other — as though you've left your present reality and reached an alternative realm, together. However, it doesn't matter how you feel in that moment; you need to approach pregnancy and parenthood in a logical manner.

It doesn't matter if your parenthood journey was planned or unexpected, or whether you're entering this world for the first time or you're having a second or third child — the best future you can give your entire family lies within good planning, knowledge, and understanding. As much as your entire body and soul are filled with a new, unique sense of happiness, you'll probably also feel some dread lurking beneath the surface. If you've had a child before, you know what that feeling is: it's the nagging fear of an unknown future, filled with worry, fear, and expectations. Any expectant parent becomes nervous, insecure, and starts doubting their own abilities. For a parent who has been through this before, you start questioning all your previous decisions and whether you did things right the first time. As a first time parent, your entire stomach has just become home to a kaleidoscope of butterflies.

You're filled with questions about taking care of your baby, yourself, or your wife, if you're the partner. These questions start rushing through your mind at the speed of light. How can you ensure your baby's safety and health in the womb, or the health of the expectant mother? How can you do your best to give yourself and your baby all that's needed? How will the delivery go, and will your baby be healthy after birth? What can you do to look after your newborn baby? How do you get through the first day? What about all the days thereafter? What do you do to successfully raise your baby for the first year and give them the best start in life?

Now, stop asking yourself a thousand questions before your mind explodes. First, acknowledge that you're taking the first step here. No matter what you do in life, you can't achieve anything without knowing how. When you started working, you didn't know exactly what to do. You had all these company policies and manuals to help you gather knowledge. You might even have attended a few training programs.

However, it doesn't matter if you have children already. A parent knows one thing for sure: every pregnancy and every baby will be different. I'm going to help first-time parents learn about all they need to prepare for. New parents will learn how to do things differently, prepare for a different journey, and even find out the reasons behind many things that need to be done.

I'm going to cover topics that will help any expectant parents understand and prepare for the prenatal and postnatal journey ahead. These topics include:

- Choosing the care provider that best suits you and your baby;
- What to expect during pregnancy check-ups;
- Nutrition, vitamins, and medical treatment during pregnancy;
- The truth behind common pregnancy myths;
- Scientific evidence pertaining to common vices, their impact, and how to overcome them;
- How to sleep when you're expecting;
- How to prepare for your baby's arrival;
- The critical first day and what to expect;
- Choosing your postnatal care provider;

- Common concerns about your baby's first-year check-ups;
- Vaccinations: why, are they necessary, and what can happen;
- Recuperating from labor or a C-section;
- Breastfeeding and bottle feeding: nutrition, common concerns, and solid food introduction;
- Bathing, diapers, clothing, and skincare;
- Need-to-know basics about your new baby's hygiene;
- Baby ailments and what to do;
- What is really an emergency;
- Creating a safe environment for your baby.

There will also be other topics. As a mother, I've tried to cover all the basic concerns you may have. My intention with this book is for you to gain confidence by learning useful information about the importance of prenatal and postnatal care up to the first year of your baby's life.

Let me start by introducing myself. I'm Harley Carr, a mother of three children aged three, five, and eight. Raising three kids is a challenging role, to say the least. I've been through a lot of challenges and difficulties during their first years of life, especially deciding whether I'll go back to work or stay at home to take care of my newborn. I chose to stay at home and became a full-time mom, and the rest is history. All of my kids were breastfed and, now that they're older, I can see the benefits of breastfeeding. I've been changing diapers for the last eight years, but I have no regrets. With the help of my partner, I've been able to survive the first year of each of my three children's lives.

In this book, I will share my insights and tips about how to manage challenges and difficulties during your baby's first year, and how to cope with the struggles of being a parent to embrace the life of parenthood. Even though I'm a mother of three, no child or pregnancy is identical. Therefore, I've meticulously searched for helpful information that pertains to this journey and I'll share any ideas that I've personally tried and tested. In addition, I've ensured that it's all the latest information, because times change and so do solutions to parenting problems.

This book will offer frank advice to help any expectant parents to become confident parents who can take care of their baby from conception until the age of 12 months. You'll learn to enter pregnancy with a healthy outlook, to cope with a newborn baby, track your baby's monthly progress, and a lot more. When you find out you're pregnant, it's difficult to distinguish unfounded concerns from reality; however, with this book, you'll learn to bridge this gap.

Enough procrastinating! Ask yourself the following questions:

- Are you prepared to learn everything, good and bad, about pregnancy?
- Are you curious about recovering from your C-section or vaginal birth?

- Do you want to learn how to take care of your newborn?
- Is introducing solid food to your baby important to you?
- Do you want to provide your baby with everything they deserve?
- Is your baby's health your number one priority?
- Do you have any doubts about your current knowledge?

Honestly, I could go on and on. The fact of the matter is, you probably only have a few months to prepare. The time will pass before you can blink, because time stands still for no person. The sooner you prepare, the faster you'll be free from prenatal and postnatal stress. What's that? You're only 12 weeks pregnant? I actually giggled there for a moment, because it doesn't matter — you need to start now. As much as I believe and encourage that you and your partner enjoy every moment, you also need to approach this with confidence, knowledge, and the tools needed to help you overcome any problems that may come your way.

Are you feeling amped now? Are you ready to go? Then say no more and continue reading this informative guide.

Part 1: Prenatal Care

Prenatal care — a foreign word, at first. If you're expecting, or even planning a pregnancy, prenatal care is essential. Half of all pregnancies are unplanned in America. I should tell you about my first pregnancy — it was an unplanned accident, but it was also a happy challenge.

I was working at the time and started feeling off. I would feel tired for no reason, and I suffered from nausea and headaches. My light bulb finally lit up when I started urinating a little more than usual and noticed my breasts had become tender. I'd been with my husband for a few years, but we hadn't discussed a baby yet.

I thought I'd test myself quietly and let him know if my suspicion was right. I was one of those women who bought three pee sticks from the drug store because I was a skeptic. I didn't have enough privacy at home, so I tested at work. All three sticks showed positive. I'm not sure why, but I refused to believe it. I went into a state of denial. I went home that night and never said a word to my darling husband.

The following day at work, I started throwing up viciously. My colleagues were concerned and called my doctor to make an appointment. My husband left work and drove me to the clinic, but I went into the doctor's office alone. I explained the three positive results I'd gotten the previous day and told my doctor that I thought they were wrong. My doctor convinced me to do a blood test and said my results would come back the next day.

I couldn't go back to work the next morning because I was suffering from such terrible nausea. However, I was feeling better later that day, and my husband took me out for lunch. As we were preparing to leave, my phone rang — it was my doctor. My husband made his way to the car before he could realize I was on the phone.

I assume my doctor didn't know how I would handle the news, because I was so clearly in denial about it. He asked me, "How would you feel about being pregnant and how would you feel if you weren't?" I was taken aback by his question but told him that I was fine either way. My doctor cleared his throat and said, "You're definitely pregnant."

The restaurant started spinning around me as the words came from my phone's speaker and I told my doctor thanks before hanging up. I made my way to the car and my husband could see that I was upset — my face was swollen and my eyes were red. When I got in the car, my husband took my hand and asked what was wrong. Somehow, I managed to tell him that I was pregnant. I remember there being an eerie silence for a few moments before he pulled me closer and kissed me gently. We hadn't planned the pregnancy, but it was welcomed with open arms.

It doesn't matter if your pregnancy is planned or not — prenatal care is essential. This is the health care needed during your pregnancy; the care that ensures both you and your unborn baby are as healthy as you can be. It's crucial that you start prenatal care as soon as you suspect pregnancy. If you aren't expecting and you're planning to become pregnant, you can start preparing your body for pregnancy before you conceive.

Preconception health can benefit you and ensure that you have fewer complications. You can prepare your body with the correct foods and vitamins, and you can quit bad habits that can harm your baby. Birth and spinal defects occur during the early stages of pregnancy, and can even happen before you know you're pregnant. Speak to your doctor about planning your pregnancy.

If you're pregnant or have any suspicion that you may be, call your doctor and start prenatal care as early as possible. Mothers who skip prenatal care are three times more likely to have a baby with low birth weight and five times more likely to have their baby die than a woman who gets prenatal care.

Your doctor can advise you on how to give your baby a healthy start in life by caring for your baby while they're in your womb. Doctors can also detect and treat health problems early on. Early treatment can cure many serious problems and prevent others.

Your doctor can also advise you on medication, treatment, habits, food, and nutrients that will ensure both you and your unborn baby are healthy. Personalized healthcare is the best option here. Something that helps other women might not work for you. Your doctor can advise you of physical exercise you may need, ways to control stress, and keep you from getting sick, which will affect you and your baby.

Your family or personal health history plays a role in your baby's health as well, and this can be monitored by your doctor. They can keep an eye for any problems due to your age, too. Beside all the concerns about health and safety, your doctor can calculate your due date or the sex of your baby — fun!

Your doctor will schedule frequent check-ups for you and you shouldn't miss any, because they're all important. In addition, they can answer all your questions.

If money is a concern, you can get assisted prenatal care by calling 800-311-2229, which will direct you to your state's family health-care center. Every state in the United States has a center to help you with everything you need to have a healthy baby (Schmitt, 2019).

I will cover prenatal care for yourself, and there will be a few tips for your partner. Let's get into the nitty gritty of it all and help you understand prenatal care.

Chapter 1: Finding the Right Maternity Care Provider and Check-Up Schedule

Choose Your Maternity Care Provider

Whether this is your first time or you're expecting your second or third child, you should gather as much information as you can. You'll want to match your own key principles for a healthy pregnancy to those of your care provider. Perhaps your family's tradition is to use a midwife or have a home birth, but only you know what you want. Your medical history can play a major role in your decision, too. Your family doctor can help you choose the care provider best suited to your individual needs.

However, there's a wide range of care providers for your pregnancy, and this range can differ from expectant mother to expectant mother. This chapter is written to help you learn more about each care provider and how they can help you.

I'll summarize research which identifies overall variances between different types of maternity care providers, such as midwives, family physicians, and obstetrician-gynaecologists (OG-GYNs). I'll focus on research published since 2005 that reports results with three or more studies to strengthen their findings.

These summaries include the best evidence and is a reliable method to learn more about each maternity care provider. In some cases, the results are old, but recent studies suggest that the results remain consistent. Let's take an in-depth look into these studies and their results so you can start deciding what you want in your care provider (Childbirth Connection, 2016).

Please bear with me through this short section, because it contains vital information and statistics.

Physician vs Midwife

Choosing between a physician and a midwife can be a grueling process. Let's take a look at recent revisions of collective studies that show the frequent advantages of midwife care (Childbirth Connection, n.d). These benefits include:

- A lower usage of fetal electronic monitoring;
- Less usage of epidural and spinal analgesia. These can be used during childbirth as a lower-risk anaesthesia;
- Little to no use of pain medication;
- Lower necessity to cut the vagina to widen it during childbirth (episiotomy);
- Increase in vaginal births after caesarean (VBAC);
- Little to no use of forceps and suction during childbirth;

- Lower cost as compared to physicians.

In similar revisions, certain concerns remain constant between midwives and physicians. The following outcome percentages show no variances between the two (Childbirth Connection, n.d):

- No tear or cut between your vagina and anus;
- Fetal distress during labor;
- Excessive bleeding of the mother during or after birth;
- Removal of placenta, as this is done by hand;
- Use of intravenous fluids (IV);
- Baby's condition after birth;
- Baby's convulsions;
- Baby's admission to a neonatal intensive care unit;
- Stillborn baby.

Certain studies suggest that you're less likely to experience the following with a midwife, and other studies say that you're just as likely to experience them with a midwife as you would with a physician (Childbirth Connection, 2016):

- Hospitalization during pregnancy;
- Higher birth weight;
- Speeding up the labor process;
- Breaking the membranes.

I hope this clarifies midwives vs physicians a little more for you. Personally, I know a few women who've had home births with a midwife and none of them have faced negative consequences. But before you make a decision, let's move onto the next comparison.

Obstetrician vs Family Physician

In some cases, you need to choose your care provider according to your medical needs or history. My friend became pregnant a few years back and was immediately referred to a specialist OB-GYN for care. She suffered from type 2 diabetes, polycystic ovary syndrome (PCOS), and a congenital heart defect. Her general practitioner knew her history, and neither he nor a midwife could help her. Her unborn baby wasn't the only one at risk — she was in danger, too. With the right care from her OB-GYN, she had a healthy baby boy six months later.

I want to share a recent review that summarizes various studies. It's old and may seem outdated, but more current individual studies are consistent with the findings.

According to research into maternity care, there's no single example of poor outcomes that can be credited to obstetrician care. Some variances have favored physicians as care providers. Physicians do well to care for women at low risk, and when they can't, they transfer women with special needs to appropriate specialized care. It's better to stick with your family physician, and obstetrician care should be reserved for high-risk expectant mothers.

Maternal care by your physician is more cost effective and convenient than having a specialist OB-GYN (Klein, 1993).

To sum up your question: the care provider you choose should be according to your needs — whether you're a low-risk or a high-risk individual, only you and your doctor can make a valid decision here. You can look at your medical history, medical conditions, traditional preferences, and your newfound knowledge combined to make a choice.

Essential Facts to Experience a Satisfying Childbirth

Quality research by Dr. George Hodnett from Bryan, Texas, who specializes in obstetrics and gynecology, has shown that four influences decide a woman's level of satisfaction during childbirth. These four influences are:

1. Having a supportive care provider;

2. Having a good relationship with your care provider;
3. Being involved in decision-making about your care;
4. Your care provider goes above and beyond to create a better-than-expected experience.

Having the right care provider makes it all seem easier and will help you deal with common fears and prevent a bad birthing experience (Hodnett, 2002).

How to Weigh My Options Before Deciding?

Your care provider will be working closely with you and your family through one of the most special and intimate journeys of your life. It's a good idea to make an educated choice. You're welcome to consult with more than one care provider before you decide.

You can also ask a loved one to accompany you to an interview when you first meet a doctor. This enables you to discuss your views with your loved one after the initial meeting. Here's a few pointers on consulting with potential doctors:

- Make sure you're prepared for the interview so you don't waste the doctor's time;
- Create a list of questions to take along;
- Explain that you're keen to be involved in decision-making;
- Make sure you meet stand-ins for your care provider because even though their stand-in will be qualified, they will work differently;
- Tour the birth location. Your care provider will have a certain location where they deliver babies.

Once you have finished your interviews, you can ask yourself the following questions:

- Did they listen to me and respect my wishes?
- Do they share my outlook on pregnancy and birth?
- Do I feel comfortable with them?
- How do I feel about this care provider?

Always follow your gut instinct. It doesn't matter how far along you are; you need to be comfortable with your decision (Childbirth Connection, 2016).

Questions for the Care Provider

It's essential to ask your potential care provider some questions for comparison of your midwife or physician. Here's a list of suitable things to ask (Childbirth Connection, 2016):

How many family members are allowed to attend the birth of my baby? Are siblings allowed? What's the age restriction?

Do you have experience with trained labor support?

How do you feel about induced labor?

When do you recommend I go to hospital once I'm in labor?

How do you feel about intravenous fluids during labor, eating and drinking during labor, and birth positions?

What do you do if labor is progressing slowly?

How often do you have to cut to widen the vagina?

What drug-free pain-relieving options do you provide?

Can I opt for an epidural?

Are alternative pain medications optional, like nitrous oxide?

How many of your deliveries have led to caesareans?

What's your approach to newborn care and what's routine for a healthy baby?

How do you feel about early skin-to-skin contact after vaginal birth and caesarean?

How should I prepare for pain during labor and birth?

What costs are involved? Do you accept my health insurance provider?

I have a certain health issue, how does this affect my care from you?

Additional Questions for the Midwife

What's your level of education? Are you certified in this state? How long have you been practicing?

Where do you attend births? Are they individual or group births? Who attends group births?

How long are prenatal visits? What happens during these visits? If there are complications, would you still be involved in my care?

How do you monitor my baby's health during labor? Do you use a fetoscope or a Doppler to monitor my baby's heart?

Are you limited to your level of care at the chosen birthing location?

What complications would require a physician to step in?

What is your procedure for transfer? Which hospital will my baby be taken to?

Are you certified in neonatal resuscitation and what equipment do you have?

If I don't have insurance coverage, what's your fee and what does it include?

Any possible extra costs I should be aware of?

Do you accept alternative payment arrangements?

Additional Questions for the Physician

What's your educational background and are you board certified?

Where do you attend births and who is present during delivery?

How does your style, values, and hospital standards compare to others?

How frequently do you suggest I attend prenatal visits?

How do I become high-risk and how will that change my care?

How do you monitor my baby's well-being? Do you use electronic fetal monitoring or do you use a fetoscope/Doppler to monitor my baby's heart?

Does the hospital you use to deliver have limits on the care you may provide?

How should I prepare for pain management during labor?

Is the hospital baby friendly and do they offer support for breastfeeding moms?

Does my baby stay in the room with me or go to the nursery?

What if I Doubt My Choice of Care Provider?

It places unnecessary strain on yourself and your loved ones if you have the wrong care provider. Sometimes, you'll need to change because your current care provider is making you feel uncomfortable, preventing you from making decisions, or your appointments are inconvenient to you.

There's no rule that says you can't change your physician, midwife, or obstetrician, but I would suggest that you consider a few things before you do.

First, make sure you have enough time to search for a new care provider. You should also search for a new care provider quietly, because some may have strict policies against this sudden change later in your pregnancy. Last, but not least, make sure your insurance is prepared to make the change, otherwise you'll have to cover the expense and the costs can quickly add up.

Don't beat yourself up for choosing the wrong care provider the first time. You're allowed to change your mind and only you know what makes you and your partner happy. The two of you should make this decision together and be comfortable and confident in your choice.

Check-Up Schedule, Test and Scan/Ultrasound

How many prenatal appointments can I expect?

The number of appointments you have to attend will depend on how far along you are. Some women don't find out they're pregnant until they're three or four months in. This isn't ideal, but it is possible. I knew a woman who never knew she was pregnant until she was nearly in her third trimester. She was used to missing her period, since she had an irregular menstrual cycle to begin with. Fortunately, both she and the baby avoided any complications because she attended all appointments that her doctor set for her.

Anyway, the average woman attends 10 to 15 appointments throughout a full-term pregnancy. If your pregnancy is free of complications, you'll need a monthly appointment from week four to week 28, an appointment every second week between weeks 28 and 36, and finally, weekly visits from week 36 onwards.

Your appointments in the third trimester increase because of a higher risk for complications. You're more likely to suffer preeclampsia — a late-stage pregnancy complication that pushes your blood pressure up, causes severe swelling of your hands and feet, and can cause your organs to stop functioning normally.

You might also have more frequent appointments if you have a history of complications or are a high-risk individual (What to Expect Editors, 2019).

What kinds of tests will I have at my check-ups?

You can expect various prenatal tests, and should just remind yourself that these are necessary. Tests you can expect at each appointment are:

- Blood pressure check;
- Weight check;
- Urine test for sugar, iron, and infections. Sugar is checked for gestational diabetes and iron is checked for preeclampsia;
- Checking your hands, feet, and face for swelling;
- An ultrasound to check on your little one;

- Your doctor will ask you about your overall health.

Some additional tests may be done, depending on your personal risk or health conditions:

- Pelvic exam or pap smear;
- Doppler monitoring;
- Glucose screening;
- Breast exam;
- Biophysical profile;
- A personal stress test.

Depending on your age, ethnicity, or family history, you may be subject to some additional tests, as well. Your care provider could run noninvasive prenatal test (NIPT) or nuchal translucency screening tests to check for abnormalities that can cause Down syndrome between weeks 11 and 13.

Furthermore, a quad screen could be used to check for trisomy 18, tube defects, and Down syndrome. Genetic abnormalities can be found in the first and second trimesters by using chorionic villus sampling test (CVS). Hence, you should discuss all possible risk factors with your doctor if there's a family history or reason for concern (What to Expect Editors, 2019).

What will we talk about?

There's a simple answer to that question: you'll talk about you and your baby. Your doctor's surely not going to want to discuss his golf game last weekend — at least, I hope he doesn't dare. If he does, please find another doctor straight away. This appointment is all about you, your partner, your baby, and your combined well-being.

Your care provider should ask you how you're feeling, both emotionally and physically. They should also offer advice for yourself and your unborn baby. You can ask your care provider all sorts of questions about your pregnancy and they should answer all of them clearly for you. In addition, they should warn you about any changes you should expect as well as changes which could indicate a problem.

It's essential for you to show up with a list of questions and concerns, and another list of any changes you've experienced. I kept a pregnancy diary and would write down my concerns whenever I thought of one so I wouldn't forget it when I saw my doctor.

Now, let's take an in-depth look at your visits (Check-ups, Tests, and Scans Available During Your Pregnancy, 2018).

First visit

If you feel nervous about your first check-up, please relax. Don't feel afraid — enjoy every moment, and look at your journey with an excited heart. After all, you've just found out that you're expecting. You know what this means? It means that you and your partner have taken a blank canvas and started creating a magnificent painting together. The two of you decide each brush stroke and color as it happens. Let's discuss what will happen at your first appointment, besides the tests I've already covered in this chapter.

Your doctor will confirm that you're pregnant and, once it's confirmed, they'll calculate your due date and determine how far you are along. You won't see much other than a little bean on an ultrasound now, but that little bean still invigorates you.

This will be followed by a full blood test to check for anemia, rubella immunity, hepatitis B & C, syphilis, chlamydia, and human immunodeficiency virus (HIV). You'll also have a basic urine test and cervical screening to check for human papillomavirus (HPV), and your doctor will check for vitamin D deficiency if you're at risk.

You'll be required to provide your medical history, current medications, smoking or drinking habits, and decide if you want a flu vaccination. These are all standard and help you pinpoint any issues that may arise or any medical conditions that can harm your baby.

9-20 weeks

This was always a memorable period for me, because something special happens during this time — you hear your baby's heartbeat for the first time. There's nothing that makes you say, "Wow, I have a life inside of me," more than hearing your little one's heart beating. In addition to this, once you see those tiny little hands and feet form, your heart melts and you find yourself yearning to hold them.

You'll have the standard run of tests that you had in the previous section. In addition, you'll have ultrasounds which will show more than a bean this time. Your baby's face and head are forming, and your baby's heart is fully formed at 10 weeks. At 12 weeks, the fetus is fully formed, and at 15 weeks, your baby can start hearing sounds. Yes, you can start talking to them now, or even playing music through prenatal earphones that you use on your navel.

From 19 weeks, your doctor will start measuring your belly and checking on your health. Some parents are fortunate enough to see the gender of their baby between 19 and 20 weeks, if you choose to find out in advance.

22 weeks

Your following check-ups will consist of all the regular blood pressure, urine, weight, and measurements again; however, your baby will start a sleep/wake pattern at 22 weeks which won't necessarily match yours. Your baby could be exploring the land of mummy tummy when you try and sleep at night, and this is when you start feeling noticeable movements. You can discuss your sleep patterns with your doctor if they're of concern. Additionally, you'll undergo a blood glucose tolerance test between week 26 and 27, and your baby's facial features will become more prominent on an ultrasound.

28 weeks

Now, you'll be required to have a few tests at 28 weeks, starting with the usual check-up tests and a whooping cough vaccination. In addition, you'll have blood tests to check for anemia, blood platelet levels, and you may be checked for HIV, hepatitis B & C, and syphilis again. If your blood type is rhesus negative and this is your first pregnancy, you'll receive an anti-D immunoglobulin injection.

Last, but not least, your care provider will discuss your birth plan and go through the basics of taking your baby home at 28 weeks. It's important to have a birth plan established so your doctor knows what you want.

Your baby is perfectly formed now and will just continue to grow. Baby's heartbeat is strong and can be heard clearly through a stethoscope. Your partner may even be able to hear the heartbeat by placing their ear in the right place — if they're lucky enough not to be kicked.

34-36 weeks

Your doctor will do the run-of-the-mill tests again, as they do with every check-up, and you may need a second anti-D immunoglobulin shot. You'll also need a group B streptococcus vaginal swab, and your doctor will assess your baby's position to see which direction your baby's lying in and whether the head is positioning itself near your pelvis.

38-39 weeks

You're nearly there now. Your doctor will check the baby's heartbeat and movement, as well as your urine, blood pressure, and your overall health, as with every check-up. If your baby's head has moved into position in the pelvis, the doctor may say their head is engaged and they're ready for delivery. Your baby's head can engage anytime between now and birth.

40-41 weeks

Your baby's genitals may look swollen on an ultrasound, but this will go back down a little while after birth. The swelling is normal and is caused by your excess pregnancy hormones. However, these should be your final appointments. I don't know about you, but I felt like I had eaten a model scale of a zoo at this stage. I was so excited for it all to be over, and I couldn't wait to meet my baby.

Your care provider will run the standard tests again. And they'll check your baby's heartbeat and amount of amniotic fluid surrounding them if you haven't given birth yet.

Chapter 2: Healthy Options

Healthy Eating Habits When You're Eating for Two

Diet During Pregnancy

A pregnant woman should correct her diet during pregnancy not to lose weight, but to give her body and her baby all the nutrients they need. You'll have to eat from various food groups in order to do this.

Let's take a look at a simple breakdown of your diet.

Fruits and Vegetables: You need 85mg of vitamin C and 0.6 to 0.8mg folic acid daily. You should have two to four fruit servings and four or more vegetable servings each day. Oranges, grapefruit, broccoli, and tomatoes are good sources of vitamin C, while lima beans, legumes, and veal are healthy sources of folic acid. One serving of vegetables is one cup; one serving of fruit is half a cup.

Grains and Breads: You'll require six to 11 ounces of this daily. It's a good source of various vitamin Bs, fibre, healthy carbohydrates, and iron. Some grains also supply you with folic acid. One serving of bread is one slice, and a serving of grains is half a cup.

Protein: Your baby needs a lot of protein. Lean beef, fish, eggs, black beans, split peas, chicken, turkey, veal, lamb, and liver contain protein, vitamin Bs, and iron. It's recommended to consume 75 to 100 grams of protein or three servings of protein daily. One serving of meat protein is approximately three ounces and a serving of legumes is half a cup.

Dairy: Good sources of calcium include milk, yogurt, cream, cream soups, and puddings.

You're recommended to consume 1,000mg of calcium daily because your baby needs plenty of calcium and will leach it from your bones if you don't have enough in your diet. You should have four servings of dairy products each day. A serving of yogurt and milk is one cup, a serving of cheese is one and a half ounces, and one egg counts as a serving (American Pregnancy Association, 2019).

Sample Daily Menu

Let's look at a sample menu I've put together for one day.

Breakfast: 1 small cup of oats, an apple, 1 slice whole wheat toast, 2 teaspoons apricot jam, and one glass of fat-free milk.

Snack: 1 cup of yogurt with half a cup of succulent strawberries.

Lunch: a hard-boiled egg with a slice of cheese on whole wheat toast, a small pack of lightly salted popcorn, an orange, and one glass of fat-free milk.

Snack: carrot sticks with a low fat cream cheese and chives dip.

Dinner: four ounces of turkey, one cup wild rice, half a cup of broccoli, half a cup of spinach, and one glass of low-fat milk.

Snack: a small bowl of freshly cut papaya or a low-fat yogurt.

Eating Seafood

While fish is a great source of protein and iron, some seafood should be avoided. The United States Food and Drug Administration (FDA) recommends that pregnant women, or women who plan to conceive, consume fish to acquire essential nutrients such as Omega 3, all ten amino acids from protein, and other vitamins and minerals. These are vitamin B6, B12, D, iron, niacin, selenium, thiamine, and potassium

— nutrients which encourage your baby's development.

However, you should avoid seafood that's filled with antibiotics, mercury, and polychlorinated biphenyl (PCB). These include fish like shrimp, tilapia, and farmed salmon. I don't advise you to eat tuna, especially canned tuna. There is a new type of canned tuna which has been approved by the FDA for consumption by pregnant women called Safe Catch Elite. The best seafood you can eat while you're pregnant is wild salmon, rainbow trout, sardines, Atlantic mackerel, and mussels (American Pregnancy Association, 2019).

Personally, I was unable to eat seafood during pregnancy and had to use an omega-3 supplement combined with my multivitamin. Seafood has a strong odor that can make it difficult for a pregnant woman to stomach.

Pregnancy Nutrition

Now, I want to discuss nutrition. Keep in mind that your weight gain shows that your baby is growing and developing in a healthy manner. To target specific nutritional needs, I would suggest that you discuss it with your doctor. Let's take a look at a general nutritional outline.

Some foods can harm your baby during pregnancy. You should always follow these guidelines (American Pregnancy Association, 2019).

- All meat products should be thoroughly cooked through;
- All alcoholic beverages should be eliminated from your diet;
- Remove coffee and sodas that contain caffeine;
- Exercise regularly.

Before you move onto the next section, I want to target some common myths regarding your nutrition.

Myth: You should be eating for two.

Fact: Yes, this is true, but your nutritional needs will only increase by 300 calories from your second trimester onwards.

Myth: If you manage your weight gain during pregnancy, your labor will be easier.

Fact: Underweight mothers place their babies at risk for premature birth, and this can negatively impact your baby's lung and heart development.

Myth: You'll crave the foods you need.

Fact: Yes, you can crave foods you need but this shouldn't be your only nutritional guideline. Besides, I craved things that should definitely not be eaten. The worst was laundry detergent. Yes, I craved laundry detergent with all my pregnancies, but I thankfully never ate any. So, no, your cravings don't always determine what you should eat. However, my detergent craving did help my doctor pinpoint my low level of iron and zinc.

Myth: If you're healthy, you won't experience symptoms.

Fact: Nausea, constipation, and heartburn will still affect you. Following a nutritional diet, exercising, and drinking plenty of water will calm your symptoms, however. It's extremely rare for a woman to experience a pregnancy without symptoms.

Vitamins for You and Your Baby

Types of Prenatal Vitamins

Although the main source of vitamins and nutrients needed during pregnancy should come from your diet (as hard as that may be some days), a daily prenatal vitamin can help fill small gaps — just in case you unintentionally don't get enough key nutrients. Prenatal vitamins should be taken up to three months before conception, if your pregnancy is planned ahead.

Remember that a prenatal vitamin, or any other supplement, can only complement a healthy diet. Consult your doctor about which supplement is best for you.

Over-the-counter (OTC) vitamins are convenient and cheaper to purchase than prescription vitamins. However, they're often made up of low-quality, synthetic mineral salts and vitamins. Let's look at vitamin E as an example. Vitamin E deficiency places your baby at risk of premature birth. OTC products often use synthetic vitamin E instead of its natural counterpart. When you read the label, natural vitamin E will read as d-alpha-tocopherol and the synthetic one will read as dl-alpha-tocopherol. I would advise that you check labels and research before purchasing any of them.

Vegan and organic vitamins usually come from organic or plant-based sources. These vitamins often come in tablet form, because the gelatin used to make capsules comes from animals. Tablets offer limited protection for the ingredients because they have no coating. They're also difficult to swallow, can cause an upset stomach, and do not absorb easily into the gastrointestinal tract. If you're vegan, you'll go for the plant-based vitamin D2, but vitamin D3 — which is derived from animals — absorbs better.

Furthermore, prescription vitamins can be prescribed by your doctor. People automatically believe that prescription medication is better than others, but the ingredients are what matter most. You should look for a multivitamin that contains enough folate, iodine, vitamin D, vitamin B, and calcium for your growing baby (American Pregnancy Association, 2019).

Why Do I Need Vitamin D?

Let's take a closer look at vitamin D. Both vitamin D2 and D3 are essential for your baby's progress, and the recommended dosage for pregnant women is 4,000 international units (IU) per day. Most supplements only have 400 IU, and an additional supplement needs to be taken.

Vitamin D supports your immune system, bone health, healthy cell division, and aids in the absorption of calcium and phosphorus. It helps your baby's bones develop, as well. However, a lack of vitamin D can lead to future problems for yourself, such as cancer, insulin resistance, heart disease, and preeclampsia.

There's a very short list of foods that contain vitamin D, like egg yolk, cod liver oil, and salmon, which is why it's essential to use a daily supplement. Another natural way to absorb vitamin D is by exposing yourself to the sun. Remember to do this in brief sessions, because sunburn will make you feel terrible (American Pregnancy Association, 2019).

Natural Sources of Vitamin B6 and Why I Need Them

Vitamin B6 is another essential vitamin to every part of your body, from brain function to producing blood cells. You can ensure an easier, healthier pregnancy for yourself and your baby by including vitamin B6 in your diet.

Vitamin B6 aids in the development of your baby's brain and nervous system, and improves your baby's birth weight. Furthermore, it helps reduce morning sickness (yay!), maintains healthy glucose levels, and helps your brain release serotonin to keep your stress levels down.

According to the University of Michigan, a pregnant woman should be taking between 10 and 25mg three times daily. However, you should avoid consuming more than 100mg per day, because this can damage your nervous system and cause numbness. With regards to your baby, the National Library of Medicine reports excessive use of vitamin B6 can cause birth defects.

Vitamin B6 is found in many dietary sources and multivitamins, so you should keep track of how much you're consuming by using a diary. Some natural sources of vitamin B6 are bananas, papayas, lean beef or pork, wild salmon, walnuts, peanuts, hazelnuts, sunflower seeds, whole wheat grains, some cereals, avocados, dried apricots, chicken, turkey, and spinach.

Most of your vitamin B6 will come from your diet, so you shouldn't need a supplement. You can speak to your doctor or nutritionist and share your diary with them. There will be signs if you need more vitamin B6 in your diet, like swollen hands and feet, swollen abdomen, fatigue, anemia, depression, and mood swings (American Pregnancy Association, 2019).

Common Illnesses During Pregnancy Like Headaches, Fever, etc.

How to Avoid Getting Sick

There's nothing worse than getting sick while you're expecting. However, prevention is better than cure, right? I want to share some tips on preventing illness from knocking down your door (American Pregnancy Association, 2019).

- Wash your hands regularly, because everything you touch can have harmful germs waiting to make you sick;
- Exercise to keep your body healthy;
- Follow a nutritious diet to build a stronger immune system;
- Use vitamins, minerals, and natural probiotics found in yogurt to aid in your overall health;
- Ensure you get enough rest.

Initial Steps You Can Take Including Natural Methods

It's a fact that even if you do everything in your power to avoid getting sick, unfortunately, the bug can still bite you and you need to deal with it as fast as you can. I remember my first time being sick during pregnancy. I wasn't sure if I was sick at first, because I couldn't tell the difference between my morning sickness and my flu. But I figured it out when my nose started spraying like a fire hydrant that's been hit by a moving bus.

Now, let's help you understand the first steps you need to take. Sadly, there's no magic trick to remove your flu — you'll need to try the usual natural methods to kick its ass.

First, you need to rest because your immune system works better when you're resting and this can help shorten your suffering. Besides rest, you need to drink plenty of fluids to help flush the bug out, and don't forget to make sure you take your vitamins, because they help your body combat this monstrosity.

Furthermore, you can reduce congestion by placing a humidifier in your room, elevating your pillow, or using nasal strips. You can also suck on ice chips or lozenges and gargle with salt water to relieve a sore throat (American Pregnancy Association, 2019).

Safe Medications

There are some medications which are relatively safe to use during pregnancy, including OTC medications which land in categories A, B, and C. I strongly advise that you always check with your doctor before you take any medication.

However, you can use Tylenol or Ibuprofen for pain and fever, you may use a low dose of Benadryl combined with Flonase spray for allergies, and you may use Vicks sugar-free cough syrup to alleviate your cough. Even though these medications are considered safe, you should wait until you reach your second trimester before using them, and always try natural methods first (Marcin & Westphalen, 2018).

When to See a Doctor

You're pregnant and it's important to listen to your body. If you've shown no improvement for days, you start feeling worse, or your symptoms are making you lose sleep or miss meals, you should see your doctor.

You should also see your doctor immediately if your fever reaches 102 degrees or more, because fever is a warning of infection in your body. If you have chest pain, wheezing, or you're coughing up colored phlegm, you may have a bronchial infection and need an antibiotic. Only your doctor can prescribe an antibiotic that's safe for you during pregnancy.

Chapter 3: Frequently Asked Questions About Safety During Pregnancy

Deli Meat

What are deli meats?

Deli meats are processed meats which have possibly been exposed to the environment and certain harmful bacteria.

Is it safe to eat deli meat?

You're allowed certain deli meats as long as the meat has been stored properly and cooked thoroughly. If you eat any deli meat, you should reheat it at 165 degrees, store it in airtight containers in your fridge for no more than three days, wash your hands after touching it, and make sure it doesn't come into contact with other foods in your fridge.

Which deli meats should I avoid during pregnancy?

Deli meats are mostly raw, however, those that have been cured and contain loads of sodium, salt, and nitrates should be avoided. Some unsafe deli items are pancetta, cured Spanish chorizo, prosciutto, ham off the bone, pepperoni, mortadella, beef pastrami, salami, and sausages. Remember to follow the guidelines on preparing deli meat before giving in to your craving for a piece of pancetta. My kryptonite was salami, because I've always loved salami.

Which deli meats are safe for me?

According to the FDA, it's safe to consume freshly cooked deli meats without preservatives or additives, lean meats that are low in fat, organic deli meats that are free from antibiotics and growth hormones, and low-salt or nitrate-free deli meats. Turkey breast, fresh deli-sliced ham, grilled pork slices, and chicken breast are safer options.

How does deli meat harm me?

Deli meat carries a bacteria called listeria and can make you develop listeriosis. Listeriosis makes you extremely ill and can even land you in the hospital with septicaemia or meningitis. Symptoms alone can be devastating to a pregnant woman, as these include fever, diarrhea, nausea, vomiting, and headaches. Why would you want to be more nauseous? Furthermore, deli meat can raise your blood pressure and cholesterol, which encourage heart problems, and the added nitrates can cause cancer (Pillai, 2019).

Pregnancy and Bed Rest

Many women dread bed rest, but let's take a look at the reasons behind it.

Why would I need bed rest?

Common reasons are preeclampsia, vaginal bleeding caused by a low-lying or prematurely separated placenta, premature labor, a weak or thinning cervix, carrying two or more babies, a history of pregnancy complications, a medical problem that was discovered by a test, or bad development of the fetus.

Am I allowed any activity during bed rest?

This depends on your prescribed bed rest, which you should clarify with your doctor. If your doctor told you to rest *most of the time*, you're allowed non-strenuous activities like bathroom breaks, a quick daily shower, and sitting in a chair or working at your desk for no more than an hour at a time. If your work is stressful, ensure that someone is close by for assistance. You're also allowed brief walks around your home for no longer than 30 minutes each time. However, you should avoid heavy lifting, sexual intercourse or activity, inserting anything into your vagina, or any activity that lasts more than an hour.

What is the best position to lay in?

Your care provider will advise you on different positions that may be comfortable, but most women prefer lying on either side. Personally, I found it most comfortable to lay on my left side or with my head slightly elevated to watch some television.

How will I get to my appointments?

Your doctor will advise you to ask your partner or a family member to drive you to their office. I had a friend who was put on bed rest and was lucky enough to have some consultations at home. It all comes back to choosing the right care provider.

How will I care for my family while I'm on bed rest?

I'm sure your partner understands how important bed rest is, and they should be reading this book with you. You'll likely need to get some outside help with the cooking and strenuous activities if your partner works full time. However, you can still spend time with your family by watching a movie together, reading a story, or playing a game.

Will I become constipated?

Following a healthy diet and drinking plenty of fluids should help. If this doesn't work, speak to your doctor about a safe laxative.

Can bed rest really make me carry to full term?

Unfortunately, there's no scientific evidence to confirm this, but many doctors believe it's the best chance you can give your baby.

Are there any side effects?

You may feel dizzy, isolated, and bored. Your body could ache in some places, too. Speak to your doctor about getting a massage therapist to help you relax your muscles.

What can I do to conquer boredom?

Besides planning your new baby's entrance into the world, you can use your computer or phone, read a book, or start scrapbooking. There are no limits on entertainment (Cleveland Clinic, 2018).

Make-Up Safety: Read the Label

Should I continue wearing make-up?

Yes, but you should be cautious, because your hormones and increased blood flow will make your skin sensitive. You could suffer from skin irritation from products you've used all your life, or notice a heat rash from the sun. Some ingredients can affect the development of fetal and postnatal growth in boys, specifically.

What should I look out for?

Start reading labels and look out for words like phthalates, triclosan, retinoids, bisphenol A (BPA), parabens, and diethyl phthalate (DEP). You should also avoid all fragranced products.

How can I prevent damage from the sun?

Choose a sunscreen with a high sun protection factor (SPF) to protect your skin. Organic and natural sunscreens have fewer harmful ingredients and make good candidates, too.

What make-up products are safe?

Personally, I didn't care much about make-up when I was pregnant, but I know many women keep wearing their favorite products. Here's a list I found online of top-rated cosmetics during pregnancy (Louie, 2018):

- Juice Beauty Stem Cellular CC Cream foundation, an organic foundation that doesn't contain parabens or phthalates;

- RMS Un-Cover Up concealer, which is a perfectly natural product;
- Afterglow Cosmetics Infused Mineral blush is 100% organic;
- Alima Pure Highlighter in Rose Gold is a great vegan product;
- ILIA Limitless Lash mascara uses natural ingredients like beeswax and shea;
- ILIA Tinted Lip conditioner is also organic;
- Superg sunscreen is a natural and mineral sunscreen.

The Effects of Tobacco, Alcohol, and Caffeine

How does smoking harm my baby?

Tobacco contains arsenic, tar products, nicotine, and carbon monoxide, which reach your baby through your placenta. Smoking and secondhand smoke can have disastrous effects, such as premature birth, low birth weight, stillbirth, the chance of sudden infant death syndrome (SIDS) is doubled, and your child could suffer from chronic health issues their entire life. Puffing isn't excluded because the smoke still enters the mucus membranes in your mouth.

How do alcoholic beverages affect my baby?

Drinking during pregnancy can lead to fetal alcohol syndrome (FAS), which causes problems like heart defects, cleft palate, intellectual disability, or physical deformities. Drinking in your first trimester can impact your baby's heart, lungs, and brain development. If you're planning a pregnancy, you should quit drinking before you conceive.

How does caffeine affect my pregnancy?

Although there's no evidence of birth defects in humans, caffeine does cause birth defects in animals. It can be found in chocolate, cola, tea, coffee, and certain pain medications. It's recommended to limit your intake to two or three servings per day to avoid potential complications (UPMC Magee-Womens Hospital, 2016).

Pregnancy and Vices

How can I boost my energy without caffeine?

You can replace your usual caffeine by eating small snacks in between your meals and exercising regularly. Snacks help to regulate your blood sugar and you can incorporate a brief exercise regimen every morning to get your juices flowing.

How do I reduce stress without smoking?

You can speak to your care provider about signing up for prenatal yoga. I joined a prenatal yoga class and it helped me calm down and deal with daily issues. It's a great idea to start a new, relaxing hobby. You could also take a baking class, take up writing, or start making jewelry.

How do I go out with someone without having a drink?

Personally, I didn't enjoy noisy, alcohol-fueled environments while I was pregnant; it increased my stress exponentially. There was one time my husband and I met with one of his high school friends and I didn't want to be the party pooper. They ordered whiskey on the rocks and I sipped a mocktail — a fancy drink that's made to look and taste alcoholic, but isn't. Ordering my mocktail made me feel like I was part of the get-together.

However, my husband was supportive and we would change our date-nights to accommodate me and our unborn baby. Instead of going to a fancy dinner with wine, we would take a walk in the park as the sun sets. I found it easy to remove this vice when I replaced it with equally satisfying adventures (Carepoint Health, 2015).

Good Pregnancy Workouts for Fitness

What exercises can I consider?

You should always check with your doctor before starting your exercise routine, but some good choices are:

Yoga and stretching exercises: This helps you release tension in your muscles and your mind. Please make sure you join a pregnancy class.

Kegels: These exercises help you to strengthen your vagina muscles in preparation for labor. You just clench your vaginal and anal muscles, hold them for a few seconds, and release. This is one exercise I still do today. You'll see more benefits of Kegels in this book.

Walking: Taking a walk in the park is easy and it can lift your mood by providing an unexpected adventure.

Indoor cycling: This is an enjoyable cardio workout that doesn't place too much strain on your body.

Swimming: This is gentle on the joints and relieves swollen ankles and aching muscles.

Water aerobics: Join a low-impact session aerobics class. Aerobics is good for your heart and lungs, and releases endorphins which make you feel good.

What should I consider in my pursuit of fitness?

Don't exercise in high altitudes where oxygen concentration is low, avoid excessive temperatures, slow your pace to accommodate your heart's pressure from your growing belly, move kindly so you don't injure yourself, and avoid strenuous sport. Furthermore, know your limits, stay hydrated, and ensure comfort at all times.

How does my fitness benefit my baby?

Your baby can have a healthier birth weight and a lower heart rate, and exercise eases labor (Johnson, 2018).

Traveling While Pregnant

This was difficult for me personally because I love traveling, but I had complications and wasn't allowed to do so. My husband was fortunate to see all these exotic and strange places, and my inability to travel seriously depressed me. I overcame my depression by reminding myself that once my baby came, I would take them to see the world and all the amazing sights it has to offer.

Is travel safe during pregnancy?

For healthy women and their unborn baby, travel is safe up to 36 weeks. However, most complications happen in the first and last trimesters, which means the safest time to travel is between weeks 14 and 28. Your doctor can tell you whether it's safe for you personally.

When is travel dangerous?

Traveling can be risky if you're carrying twins or triplets, have preeclampsia, a prelabor rupture of the membranes, or other health complications, or you have a history of complications during pregnancy.

Where should I avoid traveling?

You should avoid any area where there is a risk of contracting malaria or zika. Both diseases are carried by mosquitoes and are harmful to pregnant women. Zika can cause birth defects and malaria can affect your health.

How can I prepare for my trip?

You can do the following:

- Schedule a check-up before you leave;
- Know how far along you are;

- Pack all your OTC and prescribed medications, ointments, and vitamins to take along;
- Make sure your vaccines are up to date;
- Choose the fastest method of travel and buy transferable tickets.

How should I travel?

The best way to travel as a pregnant woman depends on where you're going.

If traveling by car, make your driving stints short, wear your seat belt, and stop regularly for walkabouts.

If you decide to fly, you should choose an aisle seat, wear your seatbelt, avoid food and drinks that make you gassy, and take a walkabout every two hours. Walkabouts help to prevent deep vein thrombosis (DVT).

If you book a cruise, make sure the ship stops off at locations with modern medical centers and has a doctor on board, and ask your own doctor for medication to help you overcome seasickness. Seasickness can amplify your pregnancy symptoms and make your trip unbearable.

What is DVT?

DVT can cause a blood clot to form in your veins, which can then shoot to your lungs. Sitting for long periods of time and being pregnant both increase your risk for DVT. You can beat DVT by taking regular walkabouts, staying hydrated, and wearing loose-fitting clothing.

When should I seek medical assistance while traveling?

If you notice any of the following worrisome signs, you should seek emergency medical care (American College of Obstetricians and Gynecologists, 2019):

- Violent vomiting or diarrhea;
- Unexplainable headache;
- A change in vision;

- Excessive swelling in your limbs or face;
- Vaginal bleeding;
- An unexpected water break;
- Severe pelvic or abdominal pain.

I know the thought of travel can be frightening, but many women travel safely while pregnant and enjoy their holidays just as much. Don't allow pregnancy to hold you back. I've always said, "Pregnancy is not a disease, it's merely a temporary condition."

Chapter 4: Pregnancy Fears and Why You Shouldn't Worry

Nausea and Morning Sickness

Morning sickness is a sensitive topic — I know it was for me. If I so much as heard the word nausea or watched a movie where someone threw up, I had to run as fast as my legs could carry me. I'm going to ask that you bear with me through this topic, if you're anything like me. If you're the dad-to-be, you might want to read this section in a supportive way and make sure your wife has a bucket handy while you do.

I want to tell you about the benefits of morning sickness. I know you might be shaking your head in disagreement right now, but there are scientific reasons behind it and benefits thereof.

Cornwell University biologists, Samuel Flaxman and Paul Sherman, confirm that morning sickness happens for a biological purpose. Flaxman and Sherman examined thousands of pregnancies before coming to a conclusion, gathering evidence to prove that morning sickness protects both yourself and your unborn baby.

Professor Sherman, co-author of *Morning Sickness: A Mechanism for Protecting Mother and Embryo*, says that morning sickness occurs at any time of the day. He refuses to call it a sickness and says it should be renamed to wellness insurance. I agree with this statement, because being pregnant is a natural part of life.

Flaxman claims studies suggest that morning sickness is your body's way of protecting itself in your vulnerable state. It causes repulsion of your food to protect you and your developing baby from toxic microorganisms and fetal organ-deforming chemicals. Your body will reject any foods containing these harmful chemicals by making you vomit or become nauseous when smelling certain foods to prevent consumption.

Morning sickness peaks between six and eighteen weeks, when fetal organ development is most susceptible to these harmful chemicals. Two thirds of pregnant women suffer from morning sickness, and the most important thing to remember is that your body knows what's best — listen to it (Flaxman & Sherman, 2000).

Let's take a look at some solutions I found online that align with my own tried-and-true methods (Reutter, 2018).

<u>Stay away from strong smells</u>. If you're cooking, open the windows and let some fresh air into the kitchen to remove pungent odors.

<u>Take your vitamins on a full stomach</u>. An empty stomach combined with iron is a recipe for nausea, and you should always eat before taking your vitamins.

Exercise helps for nausea, too. Yes, this may come as a surprise, but getting on your feet and exercising your nausea away can make you feel a lot better.

Calm your nausea with ginger. You can eat ginger preserve or drink some ginger tea. This helped me on many occasions.

Listen to your body. Avoid greasy, sweet, and spicy foods. You should be eating high carbohydrates, high protein, and bland foods to reduce nausea. Wait until you've finished eating before you drink any fluids, and leave that new Portuguese restaurant for a time when spices don't upset your stomach.

Prepare smaller meals and snacks. Don't eat three large meals daily, aim to eat six small meals, instead. You can also keep tiny snacks at your bedside in case you wake up feeling sick.

Buy yourself scented oils. I used to love scented oil over a burning candle. The smell of orange worked for me, but you can also try lavender, lemon, mint, or whatever scent floats your boat.

<u>If natural methods fail, you can turn to OTC medications</u>. Vitamin B6 reduces nausea, but please beware of an overdose. Furthermore, you can take three 25mg Benadryl a day; it's an antihistamine which is safe and helps for nausea. Please don't take this while driving, however, because it will make you drowsy.

There are worrisome signs that you may experience, and you should visit your doctor if you do.

- Dehydration, dizziness, infrequent urination, and dark or smelly urine;
- Bloody or excessive vomit;
- Abdominal or pelvic pains;
- Sudden weight loss;
- Inability to keep your food down for 12 hours or more.

I know we're all different, but I would like to share my remedy for morning sickness. I'm stubborn as an ox and never used to listen to my body. I refused to give in to my nausea with my first pregnancy and suffered the consequences. Fortunately, with my second, I met a wonderful friend who gave me sound advice — she told me to visit a hypnotherapist. It took a few rigorous sessions, but hypnosis managed to alter my way of thinking and I started listening to my body. My second and third pregnancies went far smoother than the first.

Other Common Pregnancy Problems and Their Solutions

Morning sickness isn't the only pregnancy issue, let's look at a few more. Please keep in mind that every pregnancy and every pregnant woman will experience different symptoms and not every solution will work for you. I will cover as much as I can. If any of the advice in this section isn't working for you, please visit your doctor pronto.

Constipation: Hormonal changes and your baby's growth restricts your digestion and causes constipation in pregnant women. Keep a high fibre diet with lots of whole grains, fruits, and vegetables, and don't forget to drink lots of water.

Bleeding gums: This happens due to swollen mucus membranes. To address this, decrease your sugar intake and increase calcium. Make sure you brush your teeth regularly and ask your dentist for an alcohol-free mouthwash. Don't forget to tell your dentist that you're pregnant if you pay them a visit.

Insomnia: Your body is going through changes and it's no wonder you can't sleep — eight out of ten pregnant women deal with insomnia. You can exercise, read a book, take a warm bath, or have your partner give you a relaxing massage before bed. My partner's massage treatments often did the trick for me. It's essential that you have a calm routine before bed.

Weird dreams: Personally, I found speaking to my husband about my dreams every morning put an end to this.

Indigestion and heartburn: Indigestion is caused by your growing baby placing pressure on your intestines. You should lie on your left side to prevent additional pressure on your esophagus and avoid eating large amounts of food at once. Some low-fat milk will also help soothe your heartburn.

Problems breathing: This is common, because hormonal changes and progesterone directly impact your lungs. Your breathing will become more labored as your baby grows and presses against your diaphragm. The best solution to this is to elevate your body when you're lying down, or to sit with a straight back so your lungs have more space to expand. Remember to take it easy — you have a whole other precious human inside of you.

Fatigue: In your first trimester, your hormones can take their toll on your energy levels. In your second trimester, your body has changed and you're carrying extra weight you aren't used to. Keep your nutrition and exercise in mind to start. Secondly, you're allowed to rest when you need to. Make sure your day isn't overscheduled and that you can either go to bed early at night or take an afternoon nap. I loved sneaking a nap before my older kids came home. Every time I had a new baby, I would sign my other children into a morning daycare program to allow myself some time to rest when my baby rested.

Edema or swelling: This is one issue that most women will suffer from. Edema is caused by excess fluid trapped in your tissue. Your growing uterus puts pressure on the vena cava and reduces blood flow, causing your legs to swell. You can reduce swelling by drinking lots of water and elevating your feet. I can still remember my husband coming through the door to find me sitting on a recliner in a cartoon-like fashion. Both my head and my feet were elevated, and I looked like a sandwich with a boiled egg between the buns. He would never question my position, though, because he knew how hard pregnancy was for me.

Leaking or itchy nipples: The expansion of your breasts causes the itch and prolactin causes leaking. Prolactin is a hormone that prepares your breasts for milk production. This is an annoying problem because it happens at the most inconvenient times. I used shea butter on my breasts to reduce the itching, and if you're concerned about the leaking, buy some breast pads to wear in your bra.

Backaches: These can be caused by the added weight around your midsection and breasts or by pressure on a specific nerve. I'll mention posture again — keep a good posture and don't sit for too long. Go on a walkabout in between long seatings. Don't lie down, as this can make it worse, and if you bend to pick something up, use your knees and not your back.

Hemorrhoids: These can be a horrible experience — you can have a small or large hemorrhoid on your rectum that may bleed and can be quite painful. Though it's common, you should avoid sitting on hard surfaces for long, do Kegel exercises regularly, and always answer the call of nature — never hold a bowel movement. If you already have hemorrhoids, you can try a cotton pad soaked in witch hazel solution or combine equal parts of glycerine and epsom salts to create a paste. Leave this homemade paste on the area for 20 minutes at a time and wash your anus with warm, clean water. Do this four times a day.

Hypertension: This can be a serious problem for some pregnant women and their babies. You can combat hypertension by speaking to your doctor about healthy weight gain during pregnancy, participating in stress-relieving hobbies and activities, and good nutrition and exercise. Your doctor can prescribe safe treatment as a last resort.

Stretch marks and itching: Your skin is stretching to accommodate your new belly and larger breasts — it's no wonder you're itching. I was lucky to get advice from my mother about this. She told me to control my itch and I'll control my stretch marks. Through all three pregnancies, I used mountains of thick shea butter tubs. It prevented scratching the itch and I developed little to no stretch marks. Scratching encourages stretch marks. Instead of scratching, apply creams and ointments to stop the itch and combat the scars while they're forming. This is an old trick that I'm glad my mom shared with me. If you have stretch marks, you can fade them over time with tea tree oil.

Little to no control of urination: Understand that your growing baby is constantly placing pressure on your bladder. It's common for pregnant women to have an accident. There's nothing you can do to prevent it, so I just accepted it. However, I didn't think it was cute when it happened, and I always wore a thin pad to catch the leak. Don't use a tampon, because this can carry bacteria and infection into your body and it won't stop the leak — trust me. Two ways to reduce incontinence are urinating frequently and practicing those Kegel exercises (Khan, 2018).

Working While Pregnant: Know Your Rights

Being pregnant at work can stress you out. By understanding your rights, you can reduce your stress and decide what's best for you and your baby.

According to the Family and Medical Leave Act of 1993 (FMLA), you're entitled to 12 weeks of unpaid leave if you work for a company of 50 or more employees in America. This act is strictly regulated by the United States Labor Law and hasn't changed, according to a review in 2017. Unfortunately, this discriminates against women who work for smaller companies, and some employers take advantage. The FMLA protects your job security, but doesn't protect it if you receive paid leave. Paid or unpaid leave can only be determined by your employer and maternity leave for men is dependent on your state and company. If you'd like to read more about the current laws on maternity leave, you can visit https://en.wikipedia.org/wiki/Maternity_leave_in_the_United_States#Current_legislation

Furthermore, I would like to give you some practical advice I found online to use while you're pregnant (Murkoff & What to Expect Editors, 2018).

1. You should use the methods you've learned to deal with and possibly prevent nausea and morning sickness at work;
2. Draw up a meal plan and stick to it no matter what;
3. Make sure you're comfortable by dressing comfortably, taking breaks when you need, keep your feet up when you can, adjust your chair, and do some light

stretching between work stints. Don't dress up in your two-piece formal suit with the buttons hurting your belly;

4. Stick to your check-up schedule and notify your employer of upcoming appointments in a reasonable amount of time. You can even give your employer a copy of your schedule;

5. Keep your stress levels down by doing what you can, when you can. Stay well rested, be organized, breathe in some fresh air while on your breaks, and ask for help when you need it.

Whether you're a new parent or a first-time parent, you have to speak to your employer. It's your ethical duty to discuss your pregnancy with them. It doesn't matter if you want to continue working or you want to become a stay-at-home mom, you're obligated to sit down with your employer and do what's right. The link I shared in this section will help you understand the legalities behind your job specific to your state so you may prepare yourself before talking to your boss.

Chapter 5: Late Term Pregnancy Comfort and Preparation

Maternity Jeans and Undergarments

It's inevitable that, as your pregnancy progresses, you'll become uncomfortable. Your baby is growing more and more each day, making you feel like you've swallowed a watermelon. Your breasts are enlarged and your pants can't close anymore. As a matter of fact, your button just shot right off this morning when you sat down. The time has come to make some changes.

I remember waking up one morning with my first pregnancy, feeling as though I'd gained five pounds overnight. I tried to lift myself, but I could feel this immense weight dragging me down like a ton of bricks. Once I was sitting up, I looked down at my belly and my mind created an image of a balloon. Not just a normal balloon filled with lightweight air, though, but a water balloon about to burst. This is when I realized I was no longer comfortable.

The first step you take to find comfort again is choosing the right maternity clothes. I'll go over two types with you, one of which isn't commonly discussed.

Maternity Jeans

Let's start with maternity jeans. The perfect pair of jeans is hard to come by, let alone maternity jeans. If you're a lover of jeans, like myself, you'll want to follow some tips on finding the perfect pair to wear during your pregnancy.

There are three major things to look out for when hunting for a pair of maternity jeans: stretch, waistband, and price. I'll elaborate some more (Shortsleeve, 2019).

Stretch: You need to try on each pair of maternity jeans to find the right one. Stretch is important because your baby's still growing. Don't buy a pair of jeans that have no stretch or sit tight now. In another week, they won't fit anymore, and your partner could gain another black eye from your popping buttons. You should also look out for a firm, yet soft and supportive, stretchy material.

Waistband: Maternity jeans come with a waistband panel that sits either over the bump, under the bump, or to the side. Under the bump waistbands give you support from below, over the bump waistbands give you overall support in your midsection but they sit high, and side panels feel more like a regular jean. Your maternity jean waistband is generally a matter of preference.

Price: Here, I want you to consider two factors. Are you going to wear them after your pregnancy, and how often are you going to wear them during pregnancy? It's unlikely that they'll fit after pregnancy, once you get back to your "perfect figure" again. There's no way you want your pants to look like a circus tent when you're pushing your baby's stroller around. Just like regular jeans, maternity jeans prices can range from affordable to "what the hell did you just say?" You deserve clothes that make you comfortable, but remember that you're going to need money for many important investments other than maternity clothes.

Maternity Undergarments

More important than maternity clothes, however, are maternity underwear. This is crucial for a few reasons. Your current underwear is going to stretch out and lose its shape with your growing tummy and bum. Maternity underwear is designed with comfort and growth in mind, and comes in light colors which make it easy to see any signs of discharge or specks of blood. Blood specks can be an indication of a problem or it can tell you that your baby is on their way.

Maternity underwear comes in low-cut under the bump or high-cut over the bump designs. Over the bump designs offer additional support and feel more comfortable, whereas under the bump designs can feel cooler during the hot summer months. Your choice between the two will depend on the season you're pregnant and the design that makes you feel more comfortable.

There are things to keep in mind if you're struggling to make a decision. Cotton underwear breathes better and is always a good choice — when your underwear breathes better, you're less likely to contract an infection. Most maternity underwear is 100% cotton. Another tip is that maternity underwear comes in a wide range of colors and types to suit your own sense of style. So please, don't allow your 70-year-old grandmother to scare you and tell you that you'll be looking for granny panties. Times have definitely changed (Fritz, 2019).

Maternity wear in general is far more stylish than we're led to believe. What matters most is that you choose the material that is best suited to you.

Furthermore, thick maternity jeans might not be the best idea in the middle of a hot summer, just like a summer-style maternity dress is a crazy idea in winter.

Now, let's look at other steps we can take to find comfort.

Methods to Make Sleep More Comfortable

Clothes are definitely not the only issue making you uncomfortable. Only someone who's had a baby bump can understand how you feel. You're exhausted, uncomfortable, overheating, hungry, and moody, and your bump makes you pee every 15 minutes. Every time I felt overwhelmed by my pregnancy, I would remind myself of our baby and how close we were to meeting them. Soon, I told myself, our baby would come and be a perfect blend of myself and the man I love. My hypnosis sessions continued and my entire outlook changed. When I felt bewildered, I would take a moment to sit back and focus on my baby's movements. Feeling my baby's baseball pitch would put a smile back on my face, even though it hurts.

Okay enough about me again. Here are some tips to help you find enough comfort to rest, because you certainly won't be getting much rest when your baby arrives. Soak it up now, while you feel like a mobile mountain (Miller, 2019).

Place your pillows correctly for maximum comfort. Doctor Christine Greves from the Winnie Palmer Hospital for Women and Babies says, "You should use pillows between your knees to support yourself and you won't roll onto your back and become uncomfortable."

I've used pillows to build a fort around myself when my husband left on a business trip. Having my knees bent and pillows at my front and back prevented me from moving from my ultimate comfort zone. When my husband was home, he would spoon me from the back to help stabilize me.

The weight of your growing belly puts strain on your posture, making you bend over unwillingly. You make a mistake by trying to correct this and lean backwards as you move about, placing unhealthy tension on your back. Your abdominal muscles weaken, which can impact your spine's stability and cause back pain. Additionally, Doctor Medhat Mikheal confirms that using pillows will keep your spine straight while you're resting.

Sleep on your side. According to the American Pregnancy Association (APA), this is the ideal position for restful sleep. Logically, your bump prevents you from stomach surfing, as I prefer when I'm not pregnant. Sleeping on your back can cause breathing issues, low blood pressure, and hemorrhoids. This fact has been confirmed by the American College of Obstetricians and Gynecologists, as well.

Exercise appropriately for your current condition. I know late-term pregnancy can be exhausting, but even short bouts of exercise will help you sleep better. You may check with your doctor and choose a method that's suited to how far along you are. When I was heavily pregnant, I would take short walks that only lasted 15 minutes. I wouldn't walk briskly, but just move along at a slower pace and take in the scenery along the way.

My husband and I also signed up for Lamaze classes. Not only did I learn to breathe better during strenuous activities like childbirth, I also got appropriate exercise. I remember how tired I felt after each class. My husband would try hard to convince me to have a milkshake before I went home, but I only gave in twice because I desperately needed a nap after class.

Stretch those legs at night. Waking up with an intense cramp disrupts your sleep. Unfortunately, even Doctor Greves confirms there's no specific reason behind these cramps in pregnancy. They could occur due to the heavy pressure in your uterus, or you could be dehydrated.

A little trick I used here is to keep a bottle of room-temperature water next to my bed for an emergency. In addition, I have a supportive husband — every night before I went to sleep, he would give my legs a mild stretch and rub to get the blood flowing.

You might have a few stretch exercises from prenatal yoga in mind. Just remember to check with your doctor before doing any stretches at this stage of your pregnancy.

Avoid any heartburn triggers before bed. Even though I've covered heartburn already, I'd like to point out that you should be aware of your triggers in late-term pregnancy. You'll know what causes your heartburn by now, and you should especially avoid eating those triggers as late-night snacks. Instead, change your meals around so you don't suffer excessively at night. If you're anything like me, you should also just forget about late dinners. By week 34, I was unable to eat anything substantial after seven at night.

Pee just before you climb into bed. Besides your baby pressing down on your bladder, your blood count goes up during pregnancy and your kidneys have to filter more fluid. This is why you pee more often.

I used a little trick with my second pregnancy. After eight at night, I would drink low-fat milk instead of water and reserve my water for emergencies only. Milk takes longer to filter through and this trick, combined with peeing right before bed, helped me a ton. There's no guarantee that you won't need to pee through the night, but you'll definitely pee less.

With these tips, you should be getting quality sleep in preparation for your baby.

Preparing for D-Day

I've added this section to help you prepare for D-day. This is one piece of advice that no one gave me, and it's easy to forget something when you're in a rush. I won't go into detail about each item, but I'll tell you how to keep a "ready-to-go" bag during those last few weeks of pregnancy. You can have one in the car and one at home.

Here's a list of D-day items for yourself:

- Your identity card (ID), insurance documents, and hospital paperwork;
- A printed birth plan which you discussed with your doctor;
- Socks and slippers, because your feet can get cold during labor;
- A soft bathrobe that's comfortable and easy to open;

- Flip flops for the hospital shower and a towel;
- Lotion or massage oil so your husband can calmly massage you;
- A spray bottle or hand fan to cool yourself off during labor;
- Lip balm to stop your lips from cracking;
- Extra pillows for assured comfort for yourself and one for your partner;
- An eye mask and earplugs to help you rest during quiet times and after delivery;
- Entertainment to keep you busy in down times and after delivery;
- Soft and comfortable clothes, slippers, and underwear for after delivery — and don't forget a separate bag for dirty clothes;
- Heavy-duty maternity pads;
- Nursing bras;
- Breast pump in case you're unwell and are separated from your baby;

- Toiletries for yourself, including a toothbrush, a hair brush, shampoo, soap, cream, tissues, and hair ties;
- A spare phone charger;
- Money for snacks and drinks after delivery;
- Medications and vitamins;
- This book and any other guide to newborn care;
- A camera for your partner.

A ready-to-go bag for your baby will include:

- Bodysuits that fasten in the front;
- An extra blanket for your skin-to-skin contact and to use on the way home;
- Hats, socks, and booties, because your newborn will get cold even when you're hot;
- Going-home clothes that you choose for the special occasion;
- Baby cream, powder, oil, wet wipes, diapers, and all the baby essentials.

Don't forget that you'll need to install your car seat correctly in your car when you prepare your hospital bags (The Ultimate Maternity Hospital Bag Checklist, 2019).

Now that we've covered prenatal care, it's time to move on to postnatal care.

Part Two: Postnatal Care

Postnatal care is the next fear you may have and it's a common one, shared among many expectant parents. It doesn't matter if you've done this before, you'll worry about all the risks that are involved in the birthing process, the first 24 hours of your baby's life, and how you'll recover physically and emotionally after labor — not to mention the concern surrounding the first year of your baby's life. I'm going to focus on providing as much information as I can to arm you with knowledge and prepare you for what lies ahead.

Postnatal refers to the moment your gorgeous baby enters the world and consists of many processes and learning curves while you get to know your baby. Your health and the health of your baby is at stake, and the best precautions you can take to ensure optimal results is to follow postnatal guidance from this book, your doctor, and the support group around you.

Chapter 6: Taking Care of Yourself

Recovering From Labor and Childbirth

This can be a scary and beautiful moment, all in one. You and your partner get to meet the new addition to your family, but you're still recovering from a traumatic event. Doctors will be poking and prodding you when all you want to do is rest and be with your family. It's the most invasive moment you'll ever experience. Yet, amidst the chaos, you'll be guided to restoring yourself to your former glory in no time.

Recovering From a C-Section

Many women believe that a C-section comes with a gruelling recovery process. Yes, I confirm that it is challenging, but it's not impossible whatsoever — and with the right care, you'll be well on your way to looking after your baby and enjoying every moment thereof.

How Will I Feel After Surgery?

Surely you're going to be groggy from anaesthesia or itchy from spinal or epidural narcotics. You'll also possibly experience nausea, mood swings, inflamed breasts, and vaginal discharge. This is normal after extensive surgery. However, you'll be holding your bundle of joy and I can promise you one thing, even though you feel detached from reality right now, you'll know it was worth it when you look down to see your baby snuggled in your arms.

How will I be relieved of pain?

You've just had major surgery, and you'll need medication to recover and cope with the pain. There's no shame in asking for more, if you think your care provider has underestimated your agony.

If you were given an epidural or general anaesthesia, you were probably given morphine, too. Morphine will reduce your pain for up to 24 hours and leave you feeling less groggy. Furthermore, you'll receive narcotic pain medication intravenously.

Once you're in the recovery room, you'll be given prescription pain medication. This can be used for up to a week and then you'll gradually transition to OTC medication. Be sure to drink lots of fluids to avoid constipation, because it can worsen your pain. Finally, you can use a hot water bottle or a gel ice pack in addition to medication.

Another note: Let your doctor know if you're itchy, constipated, or nauseous and they'll give you medication to reduce these issues.

When does breastfeeding start after surgery?

Breastfeeding can commence a half-hour after surgery, whether you're in the recovery room yet or not. I will cover breastfeeding extensively in chapter eight.

What are the first few days like in recovery?

You can most definitely expect a busy day. A nurse will stop in every few hours to check your vital signs, the amount of vaginal bleeding, and feel your stomach to check whether your uterus is firming. Your body will be discharging lochia, which is a vaginal discharge every new mother experiences. This bright red discharge consists of bacteria and tissue from your uterus lining — some people call this afterbirth.

Your nurse will remove your catheter and IV line within 12 hours. She'll also instruct you on how to cough and help you with deep breathing exercises to avoid fluid build-up on your lungs and prevent pneumonia. In addition, your doctor will check on your wound daily and your nurse will help you get up and walk around. Walking is essential because you need to keep your circulation flowing to avoid blood clots. You can also roll your ankles, wiggle your toes, or have your partner do a circulation massage.

Something nurses often forget to tell you is that you need to walk straight. My friend had two C-sections and with her first, she was uneducated and suffered the consequences. She forgot to mention her allergies and they covered her drainage hole with a plaster that contained an ingredient that she was allergic to, leading to septic complications. That was her own fault. However, neither her nurse or doctor corrected her posture as she bent over when she walked. Her wound took longer to heal because of the infection, and she wasn't walking upright. You're not supposed to stretch excessively, but you do have to walk straight after a C-section. Her road to recovery was long and treacherous with her first child.

Anyway, walking will help your digestive system as well, because your intestines are listless after surgery which can cause gas and bloating. In addition, you should empty your bladder often so your uterus stays contracted and doesn't add pressure to your wound. Take short walks after you've taken your pain meds.

Your doctor will also prescribe some stool softeners, some form of simethicone for gas, any vaccines you've missed, and they'll discuss birth control options with you.

What's recovery like when I leave the hospital?

You're recovering from surgery while taking care of a newborn — admit it, you need help. Make sure your partner, family, friends or even hired help are around for you during your recovery time. Don't lift anything heavier than your baby, and give your incision time to heal. Medications will help, and your incision may start feeling better after a few days. However, it can remain tender for a few months.

Your doctor will give you instructions on wound care, but you can use antibacterial soap and warm water to clean it daily. Do this in the shower but don't submerge yourself in water for the first six weeks, as this could lead to an infection. Your wound should be dried properly after cleaning. You'll most likely have dissolvable stitches, otherwise your doctor will remove the metal staples a week later.

Your vaginal discharge should gradually turn from dark red to pink and finally to yellow/white. If your bleeding returns or you have menstrual cramps, you should see your doctor. Whatever you do, don't use tampons until your six-week check-up. Even then, you can only use them with the consent of your doctor.

How active should I be during recovery?

You should continue walking, but only return to moderate exercise and sexual intercourse after six to eight weeks. In addition, don't do any strenuous housework or lifting for eight weeks. Even sweeping the floor is more strenuous than you may think. You can drive after two weeks if you aren't taking sedative pain medication and as long as you feel no discomfort from checking your blind spots, depressing the pedals, or turning the wheel. Finally, you can return to work in six to eight weeks, if your work isn't physically strenuous.

What will my C-section scar be like?

Your scar will look darker than your skin and bulge out at first, however, the bulge will grow smaller within six weeks. It will be a low-lying scar which will sit just below your pubic hair line and eventually, you'll hardly notice it — don't concern yourself with the tales you've heard of massive scars on your lower abdomen.

If your incision becomes warm and red, swells, or oozes, you need medical attention. Other common signs of infection are feeling feverish, sudden or worsening pain, smelly discharge, and burning urine.

What should I expect emotionally?

A C-section isn't to be taken lightly. There are various reasons you may have one — you could have been in labor for many hours before you were rushed to surgery, leaving you either disappointed or feeling cheated, or you might even feel relieved. It depends on your outlook and reason.

However, it's easy for frustration to take hold, because your recovery undoubtedly feels endless at first. You can only listen to your doctor's advice and follow a healthy diet.

Furthermore, it's common to have the blues after a C-section. These sneaky feelings of sadness come on about three days after your surgery and last for days. However, you should seek help if you think they're getting worse or have persisted for too long. Postnatal depression is serious and needs urgent treatment (Boyd-Barrett & Alrahmani, 2019).

Recovering From a Vaginal Birth

Why do I keep urinating so much?

Your body stored a lot of excess fluid while you were pregnant, and now it has to go somewhere. You'll urinate more frequently and have stronger, lengthier streams. It will take a few days for the excess fluid to exit your body, and you may notice swelling in your hands and feet that is worse than when you were pregnant. It's important that you stay hydrated, because your kidneys need a constant flow of fresh water to flush any toxins out.

Is it normal to leak when I cough or laugh?

Your pelvic muscles are weak from labor — this is called stress incontinence. You may not feel much in your pelvic area for about a week. Don't be embarrassed, and remember to wear your maternity pads to absorb the unexpected splash.

I used many packs of maternity pads to avoid embarrassment. I'll advise you to continue your Kegel exercises to strengthen your pelvic muscles again, but if your incontinence persists longer than two weeks, consult your doctor.

Why am I getting stomach cramps after delivery?

The pains you're feeling are contractions from your uterus. Remember, your uterus stretched up to 20 times its normal size during pregnancy, and now it has to shrink back down again. Your doctor will feel your uterus at each check-up and should no longer be able to feel it at six weeks postpartum. However, if the pressure from your doctor's hand hurts you, it could indicate an infection.

Why is my belly still big?

Your stomach doesn't magically flatten after delivery because your muscles are stretched, tired, and weak. You need to follow a healthy diet and start a more vigorous exercise regimen.

Remember to listen to your body and only push it as far as it can go, because you're still healing. You can also discuss exercises that target your stomach with a fitness specialist. Personally, I conveniently joined a postnatal exercise group at the same place we attended our Lamaze classes.

Why does it hurt to sit?

Many women experience a small tear between their vagina and anus during delivery. Occasionally, your doctor or midwife will cut you if you aren't wide enough for your baby to exit through. Some women need stitches, and a few lucky women don't. Clean your wound regularly with warm antibacterial soap water and keep it dry. Furthermore, you may use ibuprofen to ease the pain.

Why are my emotions all over the place?

Whether you're a new mother or a first-time mother, your body and hormones have gone through changes — you're sleep deprived, worried about bonding with your baby, nervous about your parenting skills, or you had a difficult and long birth. You're allowed to have the baby blues. However, if you find it difficult to cope and can't take care of your baby, speak to your partner or doctor to find help straight away.

How can I cope when I'm feeling exhausted?

Whether you've done this before or not, you know you can ask for help. Nine months of physical changes during pregnancy, your body trying to correct itself in a few weeks, and dealing with the stresses of a newborn baby can affect anyone. Reaching out for help isn't a crime (Recovery After Vaginal Birth, 2017).

Adapting to Your New Lifestyle

According to Dr. William Dement, a sleep specialist, parents lose an average of two hours of sleep per night for the first five months — with this in mind, let's look at practical advice for you to gain more sleep.

- Have a network of friends, family, and your partner on speed dial for times you need help.
- Alter your baby's environment to get them to sleep so that you can sleep. You can switch the television off, dim the lights, and close your curtains. As your baby's biological clock matures, they'll fall asleep easier.
- A trick I used with two of my children was to put them in their car seat and drive around the block a few times. The car's vibrations lulled them to sleep — and still does.
- If you can afford one, hire a domestic worker to take care of any strenuous activity that exhausts you.
- You can catch up on your own sleep by sleeping when your baby does. Make sure your environment is dimly lit, a well-

controlled temperature, and avoid stimulants like caffeine and coffee. Don't forget to switch your phone off, because your baby will wake you up like an alarm when needed. This is how I often got extra sleep in.

What do I do when I can't sleep?

Without sufficient rest, you won't cope — and that's a fact. I didn't just use hypnosis throughout my pregnancy; I listened to many relaxing self-hypnosis videos on YouTube to help me calm myself into drowsiness. If you don't want to follow a guided meditation, you can just sit back and picture yourself on a beach while you focus on your breathing. If all else fails, go to another room and read a book for a few minutes before trying to sleep again (Ding, 2019).

Getting Comfortable With Chaos

I want to share some practical advice about coping with your newfound chaos because, let's face it — your life will be chaotic now (Avery, 2018).

- Realize that this chaos is only temporary. Your house *will* be clean again, and you should only worry about your baby and enjoy every moment that you share. Your standards for a clean house can be readjusted again later.
- Speak to other parents to gather advice, whether you're new to parenting or just want some fresh opinions. Trust your instincts and filter the advice you get to best suit you.
- Communication between parents is essential to get through this chaotic stage. Tell your partner about your day, even the little things.

- As a stay-at-home mom, I cooked dinner in the morning because if the day became chaotic, I'd feel better knowing I already planned ahead.
- Don't be humble; acknowledge your hard work. Your partner can take you for a nice dinner to show appreciation for your effort.
- Lastly, get out of the house. You can't clear your mind if you're cooped up in chaos. Take your baby and have a lovely stroll in a quiet park where you can both relax and breathe in the fresh air.

Adjusting to Your Role and Handling New Baby Stress

Now it's time to accept that you're a parent for the first time or once more by reading some advice about handling new baby stress from experienced people (11 Ways to Handle New Baby Stress, 2018).

- You've already taken the first step in preparation by reading this book. The more you prepare, the less you'll be overwhelmed.
- Work as a team. Both parents should plan postnatal schedules together. Divide and conquer all plans, tasks, and decisions.
- Don't fret about your baby each time they cry. It will take you some time to grow accustomed to their cries and the meaning behind each one, and you'll learn to know every sound by heart. Besides, your baby's more resilient than you think — and so are you.
- When you bring your newborn home, you can never have enough essentials. Stockpile any diapers, medications, and toiletries you need as they go on sale.
- Allow yourself some 'you' time. One parent can watch the baby or a nanny can come over. Get out and have some fun together, because you both need and deserve it.

- Keep your camera handy because you don't know when something happens that's going to go viral.
- Don't criticize or compare yourself, your partner, your parenting skills, or your baby to another — everyone is unique and comes with their own strengths and weaknesses.
- Become a huggy-bear. Hug your partner, your mother, your brother, your friend, and, most importantly, your baby. There's a special kind of comfort that comes from hugging another person.

Chapter 7: Baby's First Days

Let's take a moment to learn about the first days you'll spend with your new baby. This chapter focuses on in-depth information about the basics, and even second-time parents can read through to find out something new by learning about the reason behind a certain test or procedure. For first-time parents, I know you're nervous, but you'll be fine. The more you learn, the better equipped you'll be. The first 24 hours is a trying time for everyone.

Baby's Appearance

Your baby will be born looking like an adorable little alien, no matter how silly that seems. Their skin will be blue and mottled, and they'll be covered in a cheesy white substance called vernix, amniotic fluid, and blood. The amniotic fluid and vernix is crucial for your baby to taste and smell when they first come out, as this helps make them feel safer in the outside world. Their skin will change to a pinkish color when they start breathing, but their hands and feet will retain a bluish hue for a few hours.

Your baby will also appear to have birthmarks on their face. Many babies are born with white, pimple-like blotches on their face that disappear over time. Some birthmarks are temporary while others are permanent. My eight-year-old has a brown birthmark on his back which looks like the Australian continent. When he was born, though, it was a colorless blotch.

If your baby was born vaginally, they could have an elongated head at first because they spent a long time squeezing through the birth canal. No one really prepares you for this and if you're a first-time parent, you'll be taken by surprise. Your baby will have soft spots at the front and back, which helped them squeeze through the birth canal. The rear soft spot takes four months to close, but the front can stay soft for nine to eighteen months. In addition, their face will be puffy, but this will change over the next few days as the accumulation of fluid and trauma of birth subside. However, your baby's genitals will be swollen, too, as you might've seen on your last ultrasound.

Some babies are born bald and some have a bush of hair. All three of my children were born with thick, dark hair. Just as their eye color changes, their hair color can change, too (What a Newborn Looks Like, 2017).

Bonding: Skin-to-Skin Contact

If you had a vaginal birth, the nurse will place your baby on your chest immediately. Skin-to-skin contact isn't only about bonding. It allows your baby to feel safe when introduced to a new world, reduces crying, regulates their body temperature, and helps to start the breastfeeding process.

If you had a C-section, you can ask your nurse for skin-to-skin contact as early as possible. This can happen in recovery with either you or your partner (Baby's First 24 Hours, 2018).

Personally, this moment was the most precious to me. I managed to forget all the pain and hard work the last nine months had been and I'd never felt closer to another person in my life. This was the very moment I felt a strong family connection to my husband and baby.

Weighing and Measuring

After your initial bonding and feeding, the nurse will take your baby to weigh them and measure the circumference of their head. Funny enough, you'll never forget these numbers for the rest of your life. Furthermore, you don't need to wash your baby for the first 24 hours.

Vitamin K

Why is it important for my baby?

Vitamin K is what helps your baby's blood clot and without it, they can suffer from vitamin K deficiency bleeding (VKDC). Although VKDC is rare, it can cause complications, such as bleeding in the brain. Babies don't get enough vitamin K during pregnancy or breastfeeding and will need to be supplemented after birth.

How is it administered?

Vitamin K can be given orally but if your baby throws up within an hour, they'll need another dose. It's absorbed better through an injection, and most hospitals will opt for a shot. One injection can protect your baby for months. If you choose oral doses, your baby will need one at birth, another at five days old, and a third at four weeks if you breastfeed. A third dose isn't needed for babies on formula because formula contains vitamin K.

Can all babies have Vitamin K?

Oral doses of vitamin K aren't suitable for all babies. Premature babies need smaller doses and it's difficult to measure this orally. Another factor is a sick baby. If your baby is ill when they need their second dose, they'll have to switch to the injection. In addition, if you were personally treated for epilepsy, tuberculosis, or blood clots during pregnancy, your baby won't be able to absorb vitamin K orally and will need the horrid jab.

Does my baby need to have it?

This is a personal preference. Medical authorities in Australia encourage all parents to give their babies vitamin K, whether they're premature or having surgery like circumcision.

Are there any side effects?

According to the Australian National Health and Medical Research Council, one study showed that vitamin K injections are associated with cancer; however, six studies done recently denied any link. The council confirms that there's no link to childhood cancer. Vitamin K injections have been administered for 30 years and there's no evidence to prove any harmful side effects.

What should I look out for?

You should watch for any unexplained bruising or discoloration of your baby's skin. If they haven't had vitamin K or need more, their blood will be thin and gather under their skin, and you should contact your doctor right away. Babies with jaundice are more susceptible to VKDB, as well.

How do I get Vitamin K for my baby?

Your care provider should ask you during pregnancy if you want oral or injected vitamin K when your baby is born. It's part of your birth plan and it will be administered after birth. Be sure to check with them and ensure that it's recorded on your baby's hospital file, even if you didn't allow a vitamin K dosage (Vitamin K at Birth, 2018).

Cord Blood Collection and RH Negative

Rhesus (RH) is an inherited protein on the surface of your red blood cells. If you're RH negative, you're missing this protein, which can complicate your second pregnancy. Your blood will be tested to see if you're RH negative. If you are RH negative and your baby is RH positive, a tiny amount of your baby's blood can contaminate yours during pregnancy or birth. Your body will build antibodies toward RH positive cells, and this can affect your second pregnancy with an RH positive baby.

Your body will release these antibodies during pregnancy and breach the placenta, dissipating your baby's blood cells and causing Rhesus disease (RHD) that can lead to brain damage, jaundice, and anemia in your second baby.

Fortunately, there's an injection you'll be offered during pregnancy to prevent this and Rhesus disease is rare nowadays.

However, if your body already has these antibodies, the injection won't help. Your pregnancy and, subsequently, your baby will need to be watched closely and a cord blood collection will be taken from your baby to test if you're RH compatible (Rhesus D Negative in Pregnancy, 2018).

Feeding and Sleeping

Your baby should latch onto your breast within the first hour after birth and keep feeding for about an hour. If they don't, you can try and coax them with some breast milk on a spoon. If this fails, speak to your doctor or a specialist nurse.

You'll keep your baby with you and, once they've been fed, they'll fall asleep. Your baby will sleep for about six hours the first time and probably half of their first day in the world.

Apgar Scores

The Apgar score is named after Dr. Virginia Apgar and is used to determine your baby's overall health one minute and five minutes after your baby's birth. This is how your care provider decides whether your baby needs emergency or medical care.

Skin color, heart rate, muscle tone, breathing rate, reflexes, and responsiveness are each measured individually. Each measurement is rated between zero and two, with two being the highest. These five measurements make up your baby's Apgar score out of ten.

An Apgar score of six or less is normal with the one-minute check-up and a score of seven or more is normal at the five-minute check-up. It's considered low if your baby's score is less than seven in the five-minute check. If your baby's score hasn't improved in the five-minute check, your doctor will watch your baby closely and treat them appropriately.

However, a low Apgar score doesn't mean your baby will have lifelong problems, it just means your baby possibly has a breathing problem that needs urgent attention by your care provider (Apgar Score, 2017).

Your Baby's First Brush With Their Senses

The first thing your baby will recognize is your voice, because they've heard it for the past nine months, and they'll respond by looking at you. They may even recognize your partner's voice, if your partner has been talking to them. Something that still amazes me is that your baby will also continue to hear your heartbeat, as they did in your womb.

However, your baby's vision is blurry when they're born, and they use their sense of sound and a 30-centimetre visual distance to recognize you. This is the perfect distance between your breasts and your face and is often called the cuddle distance.

Furthermore, your baby will taste and smell your milk and amniotic fluid, which is familiar to them (Baby's First 24 Hours, 2018).

Urine and Meconium

Your baby will pass urine and newborn poop, or meconium, at least once. Your baby's poo will change color and consistency over the next few days, but meconium is commonly seen as a black, sticky poo.

Newborn Issues

Jaundice

Jaundice is a yellowing of the skin and eyes and is rather common in babies. Your baby's jaundice may go away on its own, or they could need hospitalization. You need to keep an eye on your baby and if they're not eating well, looking more yellow, or urinating less, they might need medical treatment.

Eating problems

Your baby will lose some weight after they're born, but should gain it back within 10 to 14 days. In the first two weeks of their life, they should have two bowel movements and soak six diapers a day. This will be a good indication that they're eating well and staying hydrated.

However, your baby's spit is important, too, and you should keep an eye on it. It's normal for your baby to bring up some food spit when they burp, but you need to look out for vomit. Vomit is more violent and more substantial than spit up. If your baby keeps vomiting frequently and the vomit is darkish green in color, you should take them to the hospital.

Infection

If your baby suddenly starts crying more often and becomes restless, you should measure their temperature. An oral temperature above 100 degrees in a newborn is worrisome. A fever is the first indicator that your baby is fighting an infection. Watch carefully for fevers, especially in the first month (SickKids Staff, 2019).

Newborn Screening Test

What is newborn screening?

Newborn screening is done at the hospital. Various tests are undertaken to check for disorders that could affect your baby's development. The disorders checked for in newborn screening can seriously harm your baby's intellectual and physical well-being. These tests also look for life-threatening conditions that could arise in infancy and childhood. Early treatment is always best.

How is newborn screening done?

Newborn screening is standard and you don't need to request it. It will begin with a blood test within the first 48 hours, and a second test could be required when your baby is a week or two old. Your care doctor or midwife will prick your baby's heel to collect a few drops of blood and place it on a special type of paper which goes to the laboratory. Your baby hardly feels this and the results will come back in two to three weeks.

In addition, your baby's hearing will be tested and a pulse oximetry, which uses a sensor on their skin, will be used to see how much oxygen is in their blood. A low level of oxygen can indicate a heart issue. Both of these tests are painless to your baby.

What disorders are included in newborn screening?

Screened disorders differ from state to state. However, most states test for the following: cystic fibrosis, sickle cell disease, critical congenital heart disease, hearing problems, and phenylketonuria. Early detection and treatment can prevent life-threatening complications.

Who pays for newborn screening?

Newborn screening isn't optional. Your insurance provider will cover the costs or, if you don't have insurance, you're looking at $15 to $150 for initial screening. Additional screening will cost more. Price is dependent on your state, but some hospitals don't charge at all.

What happens if a newborn screening test comes back negative?

A negative result means your baby has no disorders checked for by the screening process. In rare cases, there could be a false negative. This only happens if the laboratory mixes the tests tubes or the screening is done too early. Don't fret, though, as this is extremely rare. A negative result means no additional testing is required, and you can take your baby back to your doctor if you notice problems down the line. Keep in mind that your care provider might not call you with a negative result.

What happens if a newborn screening test comes back positive?

A positive result means that one or more of the tests came back abnormal. A positive result doesn't guarantee that your baby has a disease — further diagnostic tests will be done. If they do have a disease, your baby will start treatment right away. It's possible to receive a false positive result as well, and the diagnostic tests will come back normal. Furthermore, your baby's results could be borderline and your doctor will need to repeat the tests.

What is newborn genomic sequencing?

Genomic sequencing is technology that determines the order of deoxyribonucleic acid (DNA) building blocks in your baby's genetic code. This technology is used to test for genetic disorders (What is Newborn Screening, 2019).

Newborn Check-Up Expectations

Check-ups are just as important to your little one as they were to you. Let's take a look at what you can expect from each visit.

At birth

Your doctor will start by recording your baby's height, head circumference, and weight on a growth chart, so your newborn can be compared to others of their age to identify any potential problems.

Your baby will have a physical examination of their ears, eyes, lungs, heart, hips, mouth, skin, abdomen, legs, and genitals to look for any abnormalities. The soft spots on your baby's head and the shape of their head will be checked, too, to see if their head is shaping well after birth.

Your doctor will test otoacoustic emission (OAE) by placing a headphone and microphone in your baby's ear to measure how sound reflects off their ear canal. They will also test auditory brainstem response (ABR) by placing electrodes on your baby's head to check the response of their hearing nerve to sound. Both tests will indicate a problem with hearing. Furthermore, a hemoglobin screening involves a blood sample taken from their heel to check for sickle cell disease, hyperthyroidism, and other inherited diseases. Lastly, your baby will receive a hepatitis B injection on their first day.

Five days after birth

Your baby will undergo another full examination on day five, which will involve a few more tests. Your baby will be measured again to keep track of their growth and feeding, have a second physical examination to look for any changes, and have a hemoglobin screening if they haven't had one yet.

Chapter 8: Baby Essentials: Feeding

Let's start with this classic face-off to decide what's best between bottle and breastfeeding. This chapter will help you understand the differences between the two and the benefits of each.

Breastfeeding Basics

The American Academy of Pediatrics (AAP) recommends exclusive breastfeeding for the first six months of your baby's life and using it to complement their diet up to two years of age (Breastfeeding Overview, 2019).

Breastfeeding provides the perfect combination of proteins, fat, and vitamins to make your baby healthy, and breast milk digests easier. It's filled with antibodies that kill bacteria, and breastfed babies typically have fewer problems like asthma, diarrhea, ear infections, allergies, respiratory illnesses and hospitalization. Furthermore, the contact allows you to bond with your baby and make them feel safe. Who wouldn't want that? The AAP confirms that breastfeeding can lower your baby's risk of specific cancers, obesity, diabetes, and possibly sudden infant death syndrome.

In addition, breastfeeding lowers your risk of osteoporosis, cancer, encourages weight loss, speedily returns your uterus to normal size, and reduces uterine bleeding. Besides, it saves you the cost of expensive formula and bottles. I'm sure you're familiar with those costs by now.

If you're concerned about your ability to produce milk, you needn't be. No matter how short your baby's feeds are, you need to keep feeding for your breasts to continue producing milk. A hormone called oxytocin sends signals to your brain to produce more milk when your breasts run low. Your first milk, called colostrum, can look a little odd. My colostrum looked like watered-down milk, at first but that's just how it looks when it starts. The color and consistency of your breast milk will change over the next few days. It's best to stick to a breastfeeding routine and your milk production will be fine.

Additionally, there are easy-to-learn positions for breastfeeding. The most important position is the one that makes both of you comfortable. Here are some helpful positions:

- *Cradle position:* Allow your baby's entire body to face you and rest the side of their head in your elbow's crevice. Keep your baby's tummy against your body to ensure that they feel secure, and support your baby's lower back by placing your free arm through their legs.
- *Side position:* This is a great option if you're recovering from surgery or feeding at night. Lie on your side with your head elevated by pillows and use your free hand to move your breast into position.

As soon as your baby latches on, you can support their head with your free hand.

- *Football position:* This is an ideal position for after a C-section, because you don't place strain on your wound. However, this is best with newborn or small babies. Lay your baby along the length of your arm, supporting their head with your palm. Your baby is supposed to look like a football.

I had trouble with my second baby. My baby's body would often hurt when held for a long time. I made use of the cradle position to prevent this and bought a baby breastfeeding sling to help. My baby soon latched on like a hungry little monster after I introduced the sling cushion.

If your baby isn't keen on feeding, try repositioning your baby and they'll latch on once they're comfortable. Then, use your free hand to cup your breast and caress their lips with your nipple. Their natural instinct is to open their mouth and latch on. Your nipple and areola should disappear into their mouth and their lips should resemble an outward sucking position. If your baby isn't latched on correctly, use your pinky finger to gently break their latch from your nipple and try again. Keep your nails short and smooth so you don't hurt their gums.

You should always follow the ABC's of breastfeeding to ensure smooth sailing.

- *A is for Awareness:* Keep supply and demand in mind here. Watch for signals that your baby's hungry or that they've had enough. Your baby will feed eight to twelve times daily for the first few weeks. Don't wait for your baby to cry, because this means they're too hungry. They'll make sucking noises, move toward your breasts, or suck their hands to indicate that they're ready to feed.
- *B is to Be patient:* Your infant will feed between 10 and 20 minutes on each breast. Don't rush them — they know how much they need. I used to divide my

baby's feedings evenly between my two breasts to avoid discomfort.
- *C stands for Comfort:* Breastfeeding must be comfortable for you, too, not just your baby. Make sure you're sitting or lying comfortably when you're feeding your baby.

Medical Concerns with Breastfeeding

Sometimes, breastfeeding isn't possible and you have to use formula. Breastfeeding isn't an option if:

- You have active and untreated tuberculosis;
- You're undergoing chemotherapy for any form of cancer;
- You suffer from human immunodeficiency virus (HIV);
- You smoke cigarettes or marijuana, use cocaine, or drink alcohol;

- You're on prescription medication for Parkinson's disease, arthritis, or taking certain pain and cold medications.

It's good to know that your baby can't contract your influenza or even the common cold through breastfeeding. However, consult with your doctor about any conditions or medications that can prevent you from breastfeeding.

Reasons Some Women Are Against Breastfeeding

You know the reasons why some women can't breastfeed, but breastfeeding is still optional even though it's recommended. There are a few reasons for women refusing to breastfeed:

- They fear that their breasts will become ugly, deformed, or sag, even though age, genetics, and smoking do more harm;
- Breastfeeding in public can be difficult and non-parents, strangers, and work colleagues can often make a woman feel

uncomfortable for no reason. Not everyone understands that breastfeeding is natural;
- They feel the pressure of having to take all the responsibility of feeding and won't seek help from their partner, friends, family, or a nanny;
- Formula digests slower, which means less frequent feedings.

However, the truth is that breast pumps solve most of these issues. Unless a woman is educated about breastfeeding, she may never learn to overcome these problems and give her baby the recommended start in life.

Common Challenges

When you start breastfeeding, you'll likely experience some difficulties along the way, especially the first time around. As a matter of fact, you may find ways of improving your method second time around, too. Let's take a look at common challenges and how to overcome them.

Sore nipples

There are a few easy ways to prevent sore nipples:

1. Make sure your baby's latched on correctly and don't tug them away. Your nipple is sensitive and tugging will hurt.
2. Feed or pump more often, because full milk ducts are painful.
3. Keep your nipples dry and allow some fresh air between feedings.
4. Start with your least tender nipple, because the baby will feed more rigorously until they're past their initial hunger stage.
5. My personal favorite is to use a warm cloth and lay back for five minutes.

However, if breastfeeding has already taken its toll on you or you're suffering common nipple issues, there are a few ways to make them feel better.

Dry or cracked nipples: If you're using bra pads, change them often to keep your nipples dry and use an unscented nipple cream daily to stop them from drying further.

Inverted nipples: I had this problem at times and would stimulate my nipples by gently rubbing my fingers over them. If you struggle with inverted nipples and can't correct them, use a breast pump or call a lactation specialist.

Engorged breasts or blocked ducts: Full breasts can cause your blood vessels to clog up. I prevented this by gently massaging my breasts once a day to stimulate circulation, no matter how weird it looked every time my husband stepped in. Another tip is to use alternating ice packs and hot showers to soothe your breasts once a day to help reduce the swelling.

Mastitis or breast infection: A breast infection is accompanied by fever and warmth. You should visit your doctor to get antibiotics that are safe to use while you continue breastfeeding. Use a warm cloth compression four to five times a day on your breasts to relieve any pain.

Stress breasts: Stress hormones interfere with your oxytocin hormone, which signals milk production. You need to be relaxed when you're feeding. I used a meditative soundtrack whenever I felt stressed during feeds. As a matter of fact, both baby and myself nodded off like this a few times.

Premature troubles: Premature babies can't breastfeed yet and you'll have to pump breast milk and feed them with a bottle or feeding tube.

However, there are some danger signs. You should contact your doctor if you see the following:

- Strange nipple discharge or bleeding;
- Your baby isn't gaining weight or filling their diapers;

- Your breasts are abnormally enlarged, painful, red, or hard.

Breastfeeding looks easy, but it isn't — and you should ask for help when you need it. Besides consulting with your doctor, you can talk with other mothers or a family member for help and advice. It's a good idea to ask a trained professional to physically show you the best ways to hold your baby and treat any problems.

Pumping Your Breasts

Using a breast pump helps a woman who can't breastfeed for various reasons. Before you start pumping, learn about the basics by visiting www.ameda.com/milk-101-article/when-and-how-long-to-pump/. Furthermore, you can read the instruction manual that came with your breast pump to make sure you're using it correctly.

Once you have an understanding of how a breast pump works, you can move on to the next stage.

Breast-milk storage

It's important to learn about storing your breast milk the right way. You can use an airtight and leak-proof glass bottle, a thick Bisphenol A (BPA)-free plastic bottle, or special breast milk freezer bags to store your milk correctly. In the first two weeks, your baby will drink 60 to 90ml per feeding, and between two weeks and six months, your baby will need 90 to 150ml each time. It's better to store individual quantities to ensure freshness and not reheat it too many times. If you're freezing the milk, leave a gap as milk expands when it freezes.

Your breast milk can survive up to eight days at the back of the fridge, where it's coldest. Label your containers and keep them away from contaminants like shellfish. Freshly pumped milk can also be kept in a cooler bag with ice packs for 24 hours and in the freezer for 12 months. However, don't refreeze milk once it's thawed. It's best thawed in your fridge and used within 24 hours (Breast Milk Storage Guidelines: How to Store Milk Safely, n.d).

Going back to work

Start pumping three to four weeks before you return to work so you can practice and build a reserve. Remember to breastfeed your baby frequently before you return to work so your body keeps producing milk. Practicing breast pumping will make sure your baby will drink from a bottle. Besides, you should stick to your routine with your baby before you go to work and as soon as you return home.

Federal law requires that workplaces have a private office or lactation room. If this weren't the case, pumping your breasts at work could be a whole lot more complicated. Your company should follow regulations, and there should be a wash basin in the designated pumping room. You'll need to wash your hands and your pump kit after each use. If you can't do this, take a few kits with you daily. You'll need 20 to 30 minutes per pumping session (Breastfeeding at Work, n.d).

Breastfeeding Health

You need to care for your own health in order to provide your baby with the best health while you're breastfeeding.

Surprisingly, you're allowed to eat anything you want, as long as you follow a balanced diet filled with nutrients. You can safely add 500 calories to your diet and eat a variety of vegetables, fruits, protein, whole grains, and healthy fats. It's also essential that you stay well hydrated and continue your prenatal vitamins.

Furthermore, don't neglect yourself or deny yourself well-deserved rest. You're most welcome to become physically active and pursue weight loss, but keep in mind, your body has gone through changes and your energy levels will be low. Remember to look after your hygiene and mental health, as well (Nagin & Shur, 2019).

Weaning

Your baby will be ready to start the weaning process at six months. They'll continue to breastfeed but will begin to eat other foods now, too. However, you should wean them gradually over weeks or months.

You can start by replacing one meal a day, moving on to two when they're doing well with the first. Keep an eye out for signals from your baby and they'll let you know when they're ready for more. Never force your baby to wean off breast milk faster than they can. Additionally, choose a new place for mealtime and avoid sitting in the same place where you breastfeed your baby to show them that there's a change happening (Weaning Your Child from Breastfeeding, 2019).

I held my baby on my lap to bond with them further and to reassure their feelings of safety after changing from lying in my arms to sitting and eating. There were a few struggles at first, when my baby would pinch my enclosed breasts, but persistence paid off well.

Bottle Feeding

Should you choose to bottle feed, this option comes with its own list of advantages and disadvantages. Let's listen to bottle feeding's argument next.

Pros and Cons

Just as anything in life has pros and cons, there are pros and cons to bottle feeding (Arora, 2019).

Advantages

- Anyone can feed your baby, giving you more freedom to finish chores.
- You can feed your baby in public without wandering eyes staring at you.
- It's easy to keep track of your baby's intake, as most bottles have

- measurements on the side and you can record your scoops.
- You don't have to follow a balanced diet (even though you should).
- Bottle feeding comes in handy for lactose intolerant babies.
- Formula has vitamin D already built into it.
- It's easier to go back to work.

Disadvantages

- Bottle feeding is way more expensive.
- It may impact your baby's immune system and they won't get the same nutritional value they do with breast milk.
- It becomes inconvenient when you have to prepare the bottle in the middle of the night in the dead of winter, or if you forget your formula at home when you go out.
- You miss out on the healthy benefits as a mother.

- Bottle feeding can put your baby at risk for certain health issues, like sudden infant death syndrome.

Okay, I know the disadvantages of formula are frightening and I agree that whenever possible, mothers should bottle feed. However, the method of feeding you choose can't be justified by anyone else.

Bottle Feeding Basics

Bottle feeding is fairly straightforward, if you know the basics. Let's learn more about formula in this section.

There's no evidence to show that expensive branded formulas are superior to cheaper generic brands. Both have to abide by FDA regulations. However, the major difference is that brand names change up their flavors and ingredients, and try to match breastmilk as much as they can (Bloch, n.d).

Let's look at some facts regarding bottle feeding in general. Some of this information is learned through experience, and I've also searched for answers through research to help you better understand bottle feeding (Alli, 2019).

1. All plastic bottles sold in the U.S. are BPA free, which means it's simply a matter of preference. Plastic is lighter and can't shatter, but glass lasts longer.
2. You should try various shapes, sizes, and flow rates to learn what your baby likes. All nipples are made of silicone or latex and should be examined frequently and replaced when necessary.
3. You can wash baby bottles by hand or in the dishwasher with hot water and an anti-bacterial detergent. However, plastic bottles should be hand-washed because extreme temperatures can cause chemicals to be released from the plastic. I'll discuss safe methods of cleaning your bottles and nipples in a later chapter.

4. Mix your formula exactly as the instructions direct. Watered-down formula deprives your baby of nutrition, can cause salt deficiency seizures, and can be tough on their kidneys and tummy.
5. You can start with a formula derived from cow's milk, soy-based, or a hypoallergenic type of formula that is iron-rich. Check the label to see whether your formula is iron-fortified. Formulas come in either ready-to-use, concentrated, or powder forms. Fair warning, my children hated soy formula.
6. Room temperature formula is perfectly fine, but if you want to heat your formula, hold it under an open hot water tap for a minute or two. You can test the temperature on the top of your hand to feel if it's warm but not too hot. Don't heat formula in a microwave, because this creates hotspots which will burn your baby's sensitive mouth.

7. Don't change formulas without speaking to your doctor. They'll be able to check for allergies from your current formula by using a simple method. Similar to the way a doctor tests adults for allergies, your doctor will place samples of each worrisome ingredient on your baby's skin and wait to see if there's a reaction.
8. Powdered formula that's been mixed can be stored in the fridge for 24 hours, opened packets of liquid formula can stay in the fridge for 48 hours, and if your formula is left out for more than two hours, chuck it.

Furthermore, here are some useful feeding tips (Alli, 2019).

1. Cradle your baby with their head higher than their body and burp them mid-feed, if they'll allow. This prevents a buildup of excess winds.
2. Don't feed your baby by allowing a pillow to support their bottle even though it

seems like the easier method when you're busy. Your baby's more likely to suffer from early tooth decay, ear infections, and possible choking if unsupervised.

3. Don't force your baby to keep drinking formula if they're finished. If they pull their face sideways, push the nipple out, or stop sucking, they've had enough.

4. Place a cloth over your shoulder before you rest your baby against it and gently rub or pat their back to release their winds. There's no need for hard knocks. Some babies don't need to be burped after feeding, so don't be surprised if your baby doesn't bring up any winds.

5. If your baby spits up a lot when you burp them, you should place them in a supportive seated position for 45 minutes. Don't lay them flat or play with them.

I'm confident that these tips have provided you with simple, yet practical advice to feed your little munchkin. Now for the next step: introducing solid foods.

Introducing Solid Food

Your baby is ready to eat solid foods from six months and will begin to show an interest in food. You can start when your baby is able to sit with support, shows good head and neck self-support, and they stop pushing spoons out with their tongue.

The order of introduction doesn't matter, but you should keep feeding them formula or breast milk anyway. You can start by giving your baby iron-rich foods like minced meat, infant cereal, mashed beans, or mashed egg yolk with a spoon. Try mixing their food with water, formula, or breast milk, and gradually thicken it over a few days. Next, start adding vitamin C, which helps them absorb iron, such as oranges, tomatoes, and spinach. Introduce a variety of soft textures including mashed, finely minced, pureed, and tender foods.

However, you should avoid mixing textures, and watch out for choking hazards like chunky vegetables, popcorn, hard candy, marshmallows or sausages. Peanut butter should also be thinly spread to prevent the baby's mouth from sticking together. Never leave your baby unattended when they're eating or drinking, and don't add any sugar or salt to their diet.

Experts advise against avoiding foods that may cause allergies like peanuts, yogurt, and seafood. Instead, you should observe your baby and immediately report any reactions to your doctor. If you introduce solid food one type at a time, you'll identify problematic foods (Introducing Solid Foods to Your Baby, 2019).

Furthermore, it's important to avoid cow's milk, as it can cause iron deficiency. Create manageable meals by sitting your baby in a comfortable, supportive position, and allow them to explore their food. Give your baby their own spoon to hold while you feed them with another spoon and let them drink from a cup.

Dish up single servings and don't allow them to eat from a container, because their saliva can spoil the remainder of their food.

Don't force your baby to finish their food when they start crying or push it away, especially when their growth is on target. Overfeeding your baby doesn't make them sleepy, so forget about that old wives' tale. As a matter of fact, an overfed baby suffers from stomach cramps and can become restless (Mayo Clinic Staff, 2019).

Chapter 9: Baby Essentials: Clothing, Diapers, Bathing, & Skincare

Now, let's get started on the second part of your baby's basic care. I've filled this chapter with my own personal experience, practical advice from other mothers, and some basic information that you may be too shy to ask about.

Baby Clothing

When to Start Shopping

Personally, I'm not superstitious and have always started shopping from the time I found out I was pregnant, because baby shopping is one thing all parents look forward to. I know there's a higher risk of miscarriage in the first trimester, but buying clothes certainly won't improve or decrease your chance of this happening. If you see something on sale, grab it. Once you realize how expensive a baby can be, you'll want to take advantage of all opportunities. If you've had a child before, you know this well.

However, you're also allowed to wait until you pass the first 12 weeks or find out the gender of your baby. It's up to you and your partner. Here are some key factors to know about shopping for baby clothes (Nishapro, 2018).

- They don't need to cost an arm and a leg.
- Your baby is growing fast, and you shouldn't stock up on items for the same age range. You'll learn to determine your baby's growth rate and buy sale items appropriately.
- Keep comfort in mind and avoid wool, lace, and frills, because your baby's skin is ultra-sensitive and these fabrics may cause irritation. Keep it simple with onesies and rompers made from cotton,

fleece, and blended materials. I first dressed my babies inside out to protect their skin from irritation from tags and stitching.

- You should set up a changing station with all your essentials at hand, because in the beginning, changing your baby won't be easy. Even if you've done it before, you'll know that it takes getting used to.
- Your baby's body isn't able to regulate temperature yet, and you can layer clothes as the temperature changes. You can also use a swaddle blanket to prevent your baby from startling themselves with their own movements by wrapping them burrito-style but not too tight.

Washing Your Baby's Clothes

Next up is washing their clothes. This information is crucial because your baby's immune system is still developing and it's easy to overlook the bacteria in your baby's clothes. Rule number one is you should always wash new clothes to avoid the harmful chemicals found in new garments. You can prepare to wash their clothes by taking the following steps:

- Read the label for instructions specific to the fabric;
- Use a chemical-free baby detergent;
- Pre-soak in warm water and soak after your wash to kill any chemicals from your detergent;
- Use sunlight to dry their clothes and avoid chemical-based dryer sheets and electric dryers;
- Avoid fabric softeners and fragranced detergents, even if you want your baby to smell like a field of cherry blossoms;
- Wash reusable diapers separate from your baby's clothes.

If you hand-wash your baby's clothes, start by washing your hands with antibacterial soap, and use infant detergent. Make sure the temperature of the water is warm and not boiling hot, and remember your soaking and drying methods.

However, if you use a washing machine, you should wash your baby's clothes before yours. You must pre-soak them with soap and use the rinse cycle twice.

Furthermore, you should disinfect your baby's clothes before you pre-soak them. Use a disinfectant baby detergent from the pharmacy to spot-treat any stains, because protein stains and bodily fluids attract bacteria. You can also add a small cap of white vinegar to your water — white vinegar also kills bacteria.

If your baby has any skin allergies, speak to your doctor about products that are safe to use (Khan, 2018).

Diapers

The next step in basic baby care is to learn about diapers. Yes, even diapers aren't as straightforward as they seem. I'm going to cover the most common concerns.

Disposable vs. Cloth

Cloth diapers are cheaper, reusable, eco-friendly, gentler on your baby's sensitive skin, and adjustable. However, they're also less absorbent, use loads of electricity and water to keep them clean, and require rigorous effort when you're cleaning them. Disposable diapers, on the other hand, are convenient, more absorbent, and come in many sizes. Unfortunately, they also cost more, aren't environmentally-friendly, are surprisingly a choking hazard, and can cause skin irritation because of gels and dyes.

Getting Equipped

There's no escaping diaper duty, but you can make it easier by preparing your essentials. Let's look at what you'll need (Murkoff & The What to Expect Editors, 2019):

You'll want to find a sturdy changing station with plenty of drawers, and make sure it's a good height so you don't hurt your back when you bend over. You can add a safety strap to secure your baby — some changing stations come with a strap installed. Next, you'll stock your changing station with diapers, creams/ointments, onesies, hand sanitizer, nail clippers, a first aid kit, pacifiers, an odor sealing diaper pail, wet wipes, and an extra change-station cover pad.

I often made my own wet wipes, inspired by a friend, and would love to share the recipe with you. The ingredients you need are:

- Two tablespoons of witch hazel extract
- Two teaspoons of liquid castile soap
- Two tablespoons of pure aloe vera
- Two rolls of heavy-duty paper towels
- An empty one-gallon ice cream bucket
- One and three-quarter cups of warm, distilled water
- Ten drops of your choice of essential oils such as tea tree or rosemary — I loved using lavender oil for this

- Optional extras include three capsules of vitamin E and two teaspoons of baby oil

Cut your paper towel rolls in half and fold them into your ice cream bucket. Mix your ingredients in a separate bowl and pour the mixture over the paper towels. Leave it to absorb for ten minutes, and shake the bucket around to make sure all the towels are soaked. Keep in mind that you should avoid using essential oils if your baby has sensitive skin.

Changing Diapers

Let's get the low-down of changing diapers and what's normal.

Urine

Baby urine is very much like yours. However, it will have a pinkish tint for the first few days — this is just a chemical reaction of your baby's first concentrated urine and the diaper. There's no need for concern when you see this.

Should your baby be urinating less or have cloudy, foul-smelling urine accompanied by a fever, you should call your doctor. Your baby should soak six diapers a day after the first week, and could be dehydrated. Fever could indicate a urinary tract infection that needs treatment.

Stools

Your baby's meconium will change to a seedy, runny, yellow poop if they're breastfeeding or soft, tan-colored poop if they're on formula. They'll likely poop up to four times a day, but this will decrease after six weeks.

However, you should watch out for red poop, which indicates gastrointestinal bleeding; black poop that can be a sign of lactose intolerance; pale or chalky poop that indicates liver problems; hard or pebble-type poop, which can indicate constipation; or any mucus in their poop. As for diarrhea, you should be aware of constant, unchanging diarrhea that's more frequent and watery than usual. If it persists and is accompanied by fever or restlessness, you should call your doctor.

Gas

Gas is normal and your baby needs to be burped regularly. This is caused by indigestion, poorly-shaped bottles, and even your own diet, if you're breastfeeding. Avoid eating gassy foods and drinking gassy sodas while you're breastfeeding.

Should your baby's stomach be bloated and harder than normal, and burping them doesn't calm them down, you should call your doctor (Bell, 2009).

Diaper Rash

Diaper rash is a common problem with babies and can appear red, tender, speckled, and raw when it's bad. Mild diaper rash will go away with simple changes.

Diaper rash can be caused by irritation from poop, urine, or even just the diaper rubbing against your baby's skin for too long, or it can be caused by allergies to skin products, ingredients in the diaper, or soaps and detergents. Furthermore, the rash could be a bacterial or fungal infection.

You can prevent diaper rash by changing your baby often and dabbing their skin with warm water. Avoid rubbing their skin, which causes further irritation. Next, you can allow them to air dry before generously adding a petroleum-based cream and, finally, replacing their diaper loosely to prevent chafing. I used to leave my baby in their crib with waterproof sheets for a few hours daily to ensure their skin stayed dry.

Should your baby's rash get worse, look raw, form pus-filled sores, or if your baby has a fever, you should contact your doctor (Tellado, 2019).

Bathing and Skin Care

Next up is bathtime basics, which is definitely another important section for new and first-time parents.

Bathing Basics

A newborn baby doesn't need to bathe daily — two to three times a week will be sufficient. Bathtime makes your baby sleepy, so you should implement a bedtime bathing routine. Start with a sponge bath before you try using a baby bath tub. Sponge baths are recommended until the umbilical cord dries up and a newborn baby boy's circumcised penis has healed.

Your baby gets cold fast, so you should find a flat surface in a warm room to bathe them. You'll need a bowl with warm water, a soft blanket for them to lay on, a soft sponge, and your essential bathing supplies. You can use the soapy, soft sponge to dab their little body clean.

Once you move onto a baby bath tub, fill it enough just to cover the bottom of your baby's bottom, and ensure your room is between 70 and 80 degrees to prevent your baby from getting cold. You can test the water with your elbow and make sure it's just comfortably warm. Place your baby in the water feet first and support their head and neck with your arm. You can slide your hand under the arm furthest away from you. Your baby will be slippery at first, but you'll learn to handle this. Don't forget that you should always support your baby with one hand while using the other to bathe them.

Use cotton swabs dipped in warm water to gently wipe your baby's eyes, from their nose to the outside of the eye. Then you can wet your soft cloth and wash their face, chin, and inside and behind their ears. Now, you can soak your cloth again and move to their neck and torso, and then down to their arms and fingers. Next, you can move down to the legs and toes.

Now you can move to their genitals. Wipe from front to back for girls, and move the foreskin back for uncircumcised boys. Use a fresh cloth with soapy warm water for this and be gentle when you wipe their genitals and backside.

If your baby has hair, you should wash it with a tear-free baby shampoo. Remember to be gentle around your baby's soft spots. If they don't have hair, you can just wipe their head with the cloth before you rinse your baby. You can hold your baby football-style again and use clean, warm water to rinse.

Now you can pat your baby dry by using a soft towel. Don't miss any folds of skin. If your baby hated his bath, you can return to sponge baths for a few days before you try again. Remember to allow your baby's skin to dry before applying the cream to their bottom (Murkoff & the What to Expect Editors, 2019).

A personal tip I'd like to share here is to use an extra towel when bathing your baby. My second child was born in the beginning of winter and there was a problem with our thermostat. When I absolutely had to bathe my baby, I wrapped them in a spare towel before submerging them in the baby bathtub and then removed the towel slowly to help them get used to the water.

Furthermore, there are some critical hygiene tips you'll need to know, which I'll cover in the next three sections.

Umbilical Cord Care

Your baby receives vital nutrients through an umbilical cord while you're pregnant, but this cord is no longer needed after birth. The doctor cuts and clamps it, leaving behind a stump which will dry up and fall off. Expose the stump to fresh air by folding your baby's diaper down in the front so it can dry out faster and allow the stump to fall off on its own.

It's normal for your baby's stump to bleed a little and crust close to the skin, especially just before it falls off. If it becomes red or swollen, oozes, creates a moist pink bump, or hasn't separated after three weeks, you should contact your doctor. This could be a sign of infection and must be treated promptly (Mayo Clinic Staff, 2018).

Circumcision Care

Circumcision is an optional route chosen by some parents. It's a simple procedure where the foreskin is removed two or three days after birth and heals in seven to ten days.

Keep the area clean by gently using unscented soap and warm water with every diaper change and allow it to air dry. Then you can smear some petroleum jelly on the tip of his penis and either wrap it with a piece of gauze or leave it bare. Gauze prevents friction caused by rubbing against his diaper, and you can even put two diapers on for extra cushioning from the discomfort and tenderness.

Your baby's penis will be a little red, there could be a drop of blood in his diaper, or you can see some yellow liquid ooze from the tip — this is all normal. However, if foul-smelling drainage, fever, swelling, fluid-filled sores, persistent bleeding, redness after more than five days, trouble urinating, or if the yellow ooze is still there after a week, you should contact your doctor (Murkoff & the What to Expect Editors, 2018).

Nail Care

Your baby's nails are sharp even though they're softer than yours. It's easy for your baby to scratch themselves when they're waving their little arms around. You should trim their fingernails three times a week and their toenails less because they grow slower. You should use an emery board for the first few weeks.

Some babies are rather fussy when it comes to nail trimming — I know mine were. You can try clipping their nails after their bath or while they're sleeping. Use baby clippers to do this and push their finger tip back so you don't clip their skin. You should cut fingernails with a curve and toenails straight, after which you should smooth out rough edges with an emery board. Ask your partner to hold or distract your baby if they wake up or become restless. I used to sing a nursery rhyme if my baby was awake and made it seem like playtime.

If you should snip their fingertips, don't panic. It happens more often than you think. Run their little finger under a stream of cold water and use a cotton swab to apply pressure for a few minutes to stop the bleeding. Don't wrap their finger in a plaster because they can choke on the plaster if they chew their finger (Montgomery, 2019).

Common Skin Conditions

There are a few common skin problems that come with babies, and you may experience one or two of them. Let's have a look at some common issues to give you an idea of what to expect (Newborn Rashes and Skin Conditions, 2018).

Pimple-like rash: Baby acne is common and will clear up on its own. It can show up on your baby's cheeks, forehead, or nose.

Blotchy skin: Some babies are born with tiny, red bumps which sometimes contain pus. This is called erythema toxicum and isn't harmful. It can appear on their entire body and should disappear within a week. In addition, African-American babies can get pustular melanosis. This rash forms blister-like pimples that break open and leave dark spots. The rash disappears a few days after birth, but the dark spots take a few weeks or months to diminish. Furthermore, your baby can have mottled skin from the cold, and you can just warm your baby up to make the 'rash' disappear.

Heat or moisture rash: A heat rash is caused by weather and overdressing your baby. You can cool your baby down by dabbing them with a wet cloth and removing a few layers of clothing. A heat rash appears as small red specks under their clothes. A moisture rash, however, is caused by their bodily fluids. Whether it's spit or sweat, it will look similar to a heat rash but can be prevented by keeping your baby's skin dry and clean.

Newborn red specks: Your newborn could be covered in tiny red specks. These are bits of blood that have surfaced due to birth trauma and will disappear after a few days.

Cradle cap: Many babies suffer from scaly and crusty skin around their head. It's an accumulation of dead cells, scales, and skin oils. It should disappear after 12 months and must be treated at home with shampoos and mineral oil from your drug store.

However, you should contact your doctor if your baby has the following worrisome signs:

- Excessive pus from any rash

- Red streaks running the area in question
- Swelling in their neck, armpit, or groin lymph nodes
- Pain or warmth in the area

On a lighter note, some common birthmarks — or angel kisses, as some people call them — are common and present themselves as a discoloration of the skin around the upper lip, between the eyebrows, upper eyebrows, and the back of the neck. Some examples are:

1. A mole is a smallish brown mark that can be hairy.
2. Mongolian spots are flat, smooth, and have a grey-blue color to them — they look like a bruise. These are common and most fade by six years old. These are likely with darker skinned babies.
3. Port-wine stains appear pinkish at birth and darken to a red-purple color over time. These are caused by underdeveloped blood vessels and can appear anywhere on your baby's body.

4. Finally, you can spot a capillary hemangiomas on your baby's skin. This can be a pink, reddish purple raised mark, or it can be flat and smooth. These are common on your baby's upper body and can grow rapidly for no reason. However, once this form of birthmark's growth halts, it starts to shrink and eventually disappears.

There are more birthmarks, but these are some of the more common ones you are likely to notice and wonder about.

Chapter 10: Care Provider and Childcare

How to Choose Your Baby's Care Provider

Getting Started

Whether or not your pregnancy is planned, you've made the first decision regarding your baby's future when you choose their doctor. All decisions are up to you, as parents, and choosing your baby's doctor is essential. You should begin your search about three months before you deliver. You can even ask your prenatal doctor or midwife for advice on choosing a postnatal doctor, or you can get recommendations from family, friends, colleagues, and parents you meet in Lamaze classes. I entered this journey with two other moms-to-be with my second and third babies which helped me a lot. Once you have a pediatrician in mind, or a few options, you can check with your insurance provider to see if they cover that specific doctor.

On the American Academy of Pediatrics (AAP) website, you'll find a section where pediatricians are listed. This is especially helpful if you're new to an area or don't have anyone you can ask. You can look at the positive and negative reviews left by previous patients for each doctor before you make your decision. Let's have a look at some other factors you'll need to consider.

Pediatricians vs. Family Physicians

Family physicians and pediatricians have the same amount of experience, but pediatricians specialize in the health, growth, behavior, and development of children up to the age of 21, whereas family physicians treat people of all ages, from children to adults and seniors (Sheahan, 2019).

Factors to Consider

Training: Is your pediatrician trained as a doctor of medicine (MD) or a doctor of osteopathy (DO)? An MD is trained in traditional medicine and a DO is trained in medicine holistically. Both are trained to diagnose and treat ailments and prevent future health issues where possible. MDs and DOs have to complete residency programs, which means they have to spend a certain amount of time doing practical work under the supervision of qualified doctors.

Choosing your doctor based on their training is your own personal preference. Every MD and DO will have to pass a difficult exam after their residency to become qualified and board certified.

Personal approach: Doctors' offices approach new parents differently — some may want a private interview and others invite expectant parents to come to their office in groups to learn more about their practice. You should aim for a private interview.

Cost: You should call each doctor's office to make an appointment and they'll inform you of any costs involved in the interview consultation. Many insurance providers pay for interview consultations.

Location: Keep in mind that your chosen doctor needs to be within close range to you. I'll tell you from experience that you shouldn't choose a doctor who's 15 miles away because if your baby chokes on something, you need to get your little one in as fast as possible. Location is vitally important.

Accessibility: On the one hand, you want a doctor who's great at their profession and on the other hand, you want one that's available for all your baby's check-ups. In my opinion, you should aim for both. My friend missed vital vaccinations for her baby because her doctor was away. His personal assistant wasn't a qualified nurse, so she couldn't help. Use a doctor who works in a partnered office or has a qualified nurse available — you can't risk your baby missing essential care.

Hours: You'll want a care provider who makes themselves available during weekends and after hours. My pediatrician was amazing, especially with my first baby. He didn't mind being disturbed after ten at night. As soon as I chose my doctor, I was given a cell number for emergencies. Little did I know, I would need it.

I will never forget my first baby scare, when I checked on my seven-month old in his crib late one Saturday night. I still tear up when I recall the dreadful feeling that came over me when I saw him. He was laying on his side with his eyes wide open when I noticed that his head and shoulders were curling backward. I felt like I was in a Stephen King novel when I saw my baby; I'd never been more afraid in my life. I shrieked for my husband to get the car keys and my phone as

I grabbed my baby and scrambled for the front door.

My baby's entire body was folding over backwards as my husband jumped in the driver's seat. I called my pediatrician immediately and he urged me to rush my baby to the hospital and promised to meet us there. After we arrived, our baby was taken away from us and we were forced to sit in the waiting room. My pediatrician arrived minutes later and reassured us that he will personally handle our baby.

We sat in the waiting area for two hours, grinding our teeth and thinking the worst, before our pediatrician came to speak to us. I remember frantically asking him where my baby was as he calmly sat me down. He had a smile on his face. He explained that our little guy was in agony from biting his tongue, which was why he was doing backflips. Besides the pain, our baby was perfectly fine.

The reason I'm sharing my story with you is because that night could have been worse — our baby could have suffered a seizure or brain aneurysm. However, thanks to our choice of pediatrician and his association with the closest hospital, our nightmare turned out to be nothing.

Interviewing Pediatricians: Good Questions to Ask

There are some questions you can ask your pediatrician when you're interviewing them to help you decide if they're the right choice for you. Take the time during your interview to notice the cleanliness and friendliness of the staff at the practice and speak to other parents who are there to see the doctor while you wait. Here's a list of the questions you need to ask in your interview (Sheahan, 2019).

Is your practice a group effort? Who will help my baby when you're unavailable?

Do you provide weekend and after-hours care?

Are you affiliated with a hospital that specializes in child care?

Can someone answer all my questions if I call your office and you're busy?

Do you always call back when I leave a message?

Do you offer video consultations if I'm away?

Do you use electronic medical records to store my baby's information?

Is there a website where I can find test results or keep an eye on my baby's developmental progress?

Will you personally handle emergencies or refer me to an emergency room?

How much are your services if my insurance provider doesn't cover costs — and even if they do, do you require me to pay cash and claim it back from my insurance?

If my baby needs specialist care, do you refer them to a specialist?

Is your vaccination policy standard with the immunization schedule of the Center for Disease Control and Prevention?

Will you be present at the initial examination of my newborn baby?

Evaluating Your Options

Now that you've interviewed potential pediatricians, you can evaluate your options. The doctor you choose will treat your baby for many years to come, and choosing a doctor that you can work well with makes you more confident and puts you and your partner in the driver's seat.

How does the doctor feel about circumcision, breastfeeding, bottle feeding, alternative medicine/treatment, and medications? Does the doctor make you feel comfortable and confident?

Will they listen to your queries and explain things in language you can understand?

There's nothing wrong with having multiple interviews and comparing notes on each doctor before you decide. Your doctor needs to match your own ideals.

Choosing Your Child Care Provider

Another key aspect of your new baby's life is choosing a care provider. Planning is how you will ensure a successful life for yourself, your partner, and your baby. It's never too early to start planning for your baby's care. You may choose to be a stay at home parent. However, placing your child in someone's care allows you to go back to work, spend time alone with your partner, and may increase your baby's learning and socialization skills. Let's take a look at the advantages and disadvantages of each type of care, as well as the average costs involved to help you prepare (Dorning, 2019).

Stay-at-home parent

The advantages of raising your child at home are:

- You decide the quality of your childcare;
- You get to raise your child with the values and traditions you believe in;
- You're there for every milestone in your baby's development;
- You get to bond with your baby every day;
- You avoid the struggle of juggling work and raising a child.

The disadvantages are:

- You don't have much support and have to do everything yourself;
- Your baby misses out on socializing and play dates have to be arranged to have them build social skills;

- You'll suffer a loss of income, medical benefits, and retirement annuities from your job if you were previously employed;
- You can become lonely if you're used to being out and about with colleagues and friends;
- You'll impact your future work possibilities — you'll have to explain why there's a gap in your resume when you do return to work.

The good news is that becoming a stay-at-home parent doesn't cost you any extra; however, the bad news is that you'll lose the income you had before.

Family care

The advantages of family care are:

- Your family member is likely to share your values and traditions;
- They have a personal interest in your baby and will provide them with familial love and attention;

- This is often a cheaper option, because your relative might refuse payment or require less compensation.

The disadvantages are:

- The way you raise a child may differ, especially if an older family member offers to assist. Their methodology could be outdated;
- Your baby doesn't socialize in this situation, either;
- You could damage your relationship with your relative because working for family can cause conflict;
- Old relatives may find it difficult to handle the responsibilities that come with a baby.

Family care can be cost effective, as most relatives won't want payment. Instead, you can pay your mother's gas bill every month to thank her for looking after your baby.

Nanny

Your baby will enjoy the following advantages:

- They'll be in a familiar environment at home;
- Your nanny is trained and experienced in modern childcare;
- There's more flexibility with a nanny and you aren't restricted to certain hours;
- It's convenient because everything your nanny needs is at home;
- Your baby will receive individual attention.

The disadvantages are:

- Unless you have a nanny-cam, you can't see what's going on;
- Play dates must be arranged again;
- Your nanny can become sick or have a family emergency and ditch you;
- There's loads of paperwork and complex taxes involved with a nanny;
- Your privacy suffers with live-in help;

- A nanny is the most expensive form of childcare.

A nanny can cost between $500 and $700 weekly, or $2,100 and $3,000 monthly. However, a live-in nanny will cost less.

Home daycare or day mother

Let's look at the advantages that come with this form of childcare:

- Smaller and more individualized care than you'll find at a daycare;
- Costs less than most childcare options;
- Your baby can socialize with other babies;
- They're normally flexible with pick-up and drop-off when you have an emergency;
- Your baby's in a home-like environment.

The disadvantages are:

- Day mothers aren't always qualified in early childhood development;

- They follow less strict licensing policies than daycares;
- They're often closed over holidays;
- Your baby's more prone to getting sick in a group environment;
- There's no direct supervision around the clock;
- Your day mother can become ill and temporarily leave you without childcare.

The cost of home daycare can vary from $300 to $1000 per month.

Daycare center

Here are some advantages of full-time daycare:

- They're reliable and won't let you down;
- Your baby is well supervised;
- Social skills flourish in daycares;
- The staff are well trained in early childhood development;
- Daycare is cheaper than a full-time nanny;

- A daycare is regulated by strict guidelines and policies.

The disadvantages can be:

- Some daycares have minimum age requirements and finding one that has space for your baby can be tedious;
- Many daycares don't facilitate sick children and a nanny will have to step in;
- Strict operating times are non-flexible;
- Closed on most holidays;
- The care is impersonal because the carer has to look after up to three babies at once.

Full-time daycare can cost between $380 and $1564 monthly.

Preschool

Preschool isn't something you need to worry about in the first year of your baby's life, but I'll cover it nonetheless. While Preschools are similar to daycares, they follow different regulations and are education-based. Your child can attend preschool between the ages of two and five.

The advantages of preschool are:

- Preschools are reliable;
- The teachers are well trained;
- Your child will improve their social skills;
- Preschools are well regulated;
- It's a structured environment with regular outings;
- Their educational curriculum is focused on your child's precise level of development.

The disadvantages are:

- Your child gets sick often in a group environment and you're not allowed to send them to school when they're sick;
- Preschools close for holidays;
- Strict hours in which you need to drop off and pick up your child;

- Each teacher attends to an average of eight children at a time.

The cost of full-time preschool currently ranges between $372 and $1,100 a month. However, by the time your little one goes to preschool, these amounts may change.

Chapter 11: Check-Up Schedule and Vaccinations

Check-Up Schedule

It's important to understand your baby's necessary check-ups to ensure their growth and development. The AAP recommends the following check-ups, which I've placed in a simple-to-understand set of guidelines for new or curious parents (Yang, 2019).

One Month

Your baby will be measured, assessed behaviorally, physically examined over their entire little body, and undergo a developmental surveillance similar to the tests done at birth. These tests will help your pediatrician determine if your baby is developing normally in comparison to other babies of their age. Your doctor will ask about your baby's sleeping, eating, bowel movements, responses to sound, movements, and their development in flexing their arms and legs.

Next, your doctor will review the screening done at the hospital and rerun any tests if necessary. If your baby's hearing wasn't tested or their screening wasn't done, they'll do it this time. Your doctor will then give your baby a second HepB shot with either this check-up or the next.

Finally, your doctor may test your baby for tuberculosis (TB). TB causes heavy breathing, night sweating, swollen glands, a persistent cough, fever, slow growth, and weight loss. Your doctor will inject an inactive strain of TB into your baby's arm and you'll wait 48 to 72 hours to see the result. If the result is positive, your baby's arm will turn red around the injection site and swell up. You'll need to inform your doctor if this happens.

Two Months

Your baby's two-month check-up isn't for the faint-hearted. Your pediatrician will examine your baby physically and check all the basics again. Weighing your baby will help the doctor determine their growth and whether your baby's eating well. But this is when the terrifying needles come out, so brace yourself.

Your baby will receive their second HepB shot if they haven't received it yet. This will be followed by a rotavirus vaccine (RV), which could be the first of up to three doses by the time your baby is six months old. The number of times your baby receives the RV vaccination depends on the brand your doctor uses. Next, your baby will receive Haemophilus influenza type b conjugate vaccine (Hib), pneumococcal vaccine (PCV), diphtheria and tetanus toxoids and acellular pertussis vaccine (DTaP), and finally, inactivated poliovirus vaccine (IPV).

I cried with my first child because I couldn't stand my baby's crying. Yes, the doctor does combine some of these shots, but it still shattered my heart into a million pieces when I watched my baby screaming.

Four Months

Even though you and your baby may be traumatized after your last check-up, the four-month check-up can't be missed. Your baby will get the regular weighing, measurements, behavioral assessment, and physical exam for their record. The doctor will continue comparing your baby's development with other babies' charts to look for any worrisome inconsistencies.

In addition, your baby will have a hemoglobin screening to check for anemia and will have second doses of Hib, PCV, IPV, RV, and DTaP. I'm sure you'll be stronger for these this time round.

By the way, my husband and I decided to attend all check-ups together after the trauma of the first. That way, we were able to support each other when we heard our baby crying, because those cries resonate through a parent.

Six Months

Your baby will go through the regular checks of weight, physical examination, and developmental surveillance for their comparison chart.

Furthermore, your pediatrician may do a lead screening to ensure that your baby hasn't been exposed to worrisome levels of lead — high levels can impact your baby's development. In addition, your baby will likely have their first tooth, and an oral check is in order. If your baby hasn't been tested for TB, they'll be tested now.

As far as vaccines go, your baby will receive an influenza shot on your request if it's winter, and they'll receive their third doses of PCV, DTaP, and perhaps Hib. Additionally, your baby may need another RV vaccination, a third IPV vaccination between now and 18 months, and a final HepB shot before 18 months.

I would strongly recommend the influenza shot if it's mid-winter, because you can save your baby and yourself from a nasty flu.

Nine Months

Your baby will undergo the regular weight, measurements, behavioral, and physical examination for their chart. Your doctor will also check their oral health again, and they may receive a HepB or RV shot if they didn't get one last time.

However, your pediatrician will perform a development screening at this time, which is more formal than previous assessments. The test will include a bunch of questions about your baby's behavior and growth. Your doctor may request that you play with your baby while he questions you, because this will help your doctor visualize your baby's behavior and movements to see if they're learning fundamental skills appropriate to their age.

This screening will help your doctor decide if your baby needs further developmental screenings. If your baby is a high-risk infant, these screenings will happen frequently. Low birth weight, premature birth, and having a sibling diagnosed with autism spectrum disorder (ASD) automatically places your baby at a higher risk.

Finally, your doctor will take a small amount of blood to check for iron deficiency and lead levels again.

Twelve Months

It's rather common for your baby to celebrate their first birthday with a check-up. Your doctor will check measurements, weight, do a physical exam, and assess your baby's development.

Your baby might receive another lead screening or TB test, a hemoglobin screening, and their cute milk teeth will be examined once more. Next, your baby will be poked and prodded.

Your baby will get their final dose of HepB and their third shot of IPV if they haven't received it yet. This will be followed by a third or fourth dose of Hib and a fourth dose of PCV between now and 15 months. Next, they'll receive their first dose of measles, mumps, and rubella (MMR) shot and a varicella vaccine now or at their following check-up. The prodding will end with the first dose of HepA vaccine, which must be administered again after six months.

Fifteen Months

I must admit, you start growing accustomed to these check-ups by 15 months. Of course, it still hurts like hell when your baby cries, but you know it's for their own benefit.

At 15 months, your baby will get all the regular weight checks, measurements, and a physical exam again. They'll also receive the HepB, Hib, PCV, varicella, HepA, MMR, and IPV shots if they didn't receive them last time. Your doctor will further administer the fourth dose of DTaP between now and 18 months.

Eighteen Months

Your 18-month check-up will comprise of the usual physical exams, weighing, and developmental assessment for record. In addition, your doctor might do a TB test, oral examination, lead screening, and hemoglobin screening. Your baby will also receive any outstanding HepB, DTaP, HepA, and IPV shots.

Furthermore, the 18-month check-up is crucial for the first autism screening. Your doctor will run tests to check for ASD warning signs. ASD can halt your baby's communication, social, and behavioral skills. This is a common screening between a year and two years in a child's life and should your doctor find a problem, they'll refer you to a specialist or program that can help your baby.

Twenty-Four Months

Wow, your baby is two years old now. Irrespective, your baby will undergo the usual physical exam, weight check, behavioral assessment, autism screening, and developmental surveillance. Additionally, your child may have a TB test, oral examination, hemoglobin screening, or a lead screening.

Furthermore, your child should receive two quadrivalent meningococcal conjugate vaccines (MCV4) eight weeks apart. This should happen between the ages of two and ten. Your doctor may also do a blood test to check for lipid disorder, which can lead to heart problems.

Otherwise, you're out of the heavy check-up battlefield and you no longer need to hear your little one scream blue murder.

Questions and Concerns About Check-Ups

You may wonder why vaccines are necessary, and I'll answer this question for you in the following section. I haven't sugar-coated the information, because it's vital for you to understand why your baby needs vaccinations. Shall we proceed?

How Do Vaccinations Work?

A vaccine teaches your baby's immune system to identify and kill bacterial or viral pathogens. When certain antigens are injected into their bodies, their body triggers an immune system reaction. Antigens are tiny molecules of bad pathogens, and your baby's body is able to react appropriately to these minimal forms of pathogens. When the pathogen reappears naturally, your baby's immune system creates antibodies and kills them.

Your baby can also be vaccinated using inactive pathogens. Even though the pathogens are dead, your baby's immune system will still identify and destroy them. A conjugate vaccine contains pathogens which have been immobilized and they can't make your baby sick, allowing your baby's immune system to safely do its thing (How Vaccines Work, 2019).

Why Should Our Baby Be Vaccinated?

The best way for me to answer this question is to provide you with a list of the many ways vaccination helps your baby (10 Reasons to Get Vaccinated, n.d).

- It will keep your baby healthy;
- Your baby's immune system is built with vaccinations and nutrition because they're born with an undeveloped immune system;
- Vaccines are one of the safest medical products in the world;

- They don't make your baby sick with the disease they're meant to prevent;
- The diseases that are prevented by vaccines haven't disappeared and you need to prevent them from happening to your baby;
- It can impact whether your baby lives or dies;
- Vaccine-preventable diseases can cost an arm and a leg;
- When your baby gets sick, they risk the health of everyone around them.

Are Vaccine Additives Safe?

Once a vaccine is issued in the United States, the FDA and CDC place these vaccinations under a microscope to ensure their safety. Many vaccines contain adjuvant, which is a specific ingredient that helps the vaccine work better by creating a stronger immune response (Vaccine Safety, 2018).

Can Vaccination Affect an Autistic Child?

A study published in the Journal of Pediatrics, 2013, proved that vaccinations in the first two years of a child's life didn't contribute to the development of ASD (DeStefano; Price; & Weintraub, 2013).

Vaccination Schedule

Now, I need you to grit your teeth as I go into some tough-to-read information.

Childhood Vaccinations

Let's have a look at common childhood diseases, their symptoms, their complications, and the vaccines that prevent them from making your little one dangerously sick (Centers for Disease Control and Prevention, 2019).

Hepatitis A is restricted with a HepA shot. It's contracted through contaminated food or water and direct contact. Symptoms can include loss of appetite, fatigue, vomiting, jaundice, fever, and dark urine, but your baby may not even show symptoms. Your child can suffer from kidney or pancreatic issues, blood disorders, liver failure, and joint pain if they contract hepatitis A.

Hepatitis B is contained with a Hep B vaccine and can be contracted through contact with contaminated blood or bodily fluids. There can be no symptoms or your baby can suffer from a headache, fever, weakness, vomiting, joint pain, or jaundice. Complications include cancer, failure, or chronic infections of the liver when they get older.

Your child is protected from *diphtheria* with a DTaP vaccine. This is contracted through direct contact and can be airborne. Symptoms include a mild fever, weakness, sore throat, and swollen neck glands. Complications include heart failure, death, paralysis, coma, and swelling of the heart muscles.

The RV vaccine protects your little one from *rotavirus*. This is contracted through the mouth and diarrhea, vomiting, and fever are common symptoms. Complications are severe diarrhea and dehydration.

The PCV vaccine protects your child from *pneumococcal* disease. This disease is transmitted through direct contact and is airborne. Symptoms may include an infection of the lungs (pneumonia), but it can have no symptoms at all. However, complications include an infection of the blood, infection of the spinal cord and brain (meningitis), and death.

The MMR vaccine prevents *measles*. This is contracted through direct contact and is airborne. Symptoms include a cough, runny nose, pink eye, fever, and, most noticeably, a rash. Complications can include swelling of the brain (encephalitis), pneumonia, and death.

The varicella vaccine prevents *chickenpox* which is airborne or contracted through direct contact.

Symptoms are headache, fever, fatigue, and rash. Complications are bleeding disorders, encephalitis, infected blisters, and pneumonia.

The MMR vaccine also protects against *rubella*, or German measles, which is airborne or contracted through direct contact. Symptoms can include swollen lymph nodes, fever, and a rash. Complications cause birth defects, miscarriage, premature labor, and stillbirth in pregnant woman.

The Hib vaccine fights against *haemophilus influenzae type b* diseases that are airborne or contracted through direct contact. This disease can present no symptoms until bacteria enters the bloodstream. However, complications include intellectual disability, meningitis, a life-threatening infection that causes breathing issues (epiglottitis), pneumonia, and death.

The MMR vaccine fights *mumps* which is also airborne or contracted through direct contact. Symptoms include a fever, headache, fatigue, muscle pain, and heavily swollen salivary glands. Complications include hearing loss, swollen testicles or ovaries, encephalitis, and meningitis.

The IPV vaccine protects your child against *polio*. Polio is contracted through the mouth, direct contact, and is airborne. There may be no symptoms, but if there are, they include a fever, headache, sore throat, or nausea. Complications are paralysis and death.

The DTaP vaccine prevents *tetanus,* which is contracted through a cut, bite, or lesion. Symptoms include muscle spasms, fever, neck and abdominal stiffness, as well as difficulty swallowing. Complications are labored breathing, broken bones, and death.

The DTaP vaccine also protects against whooping cough, or *pertussis*. Pertussis is contracted through direct contact and is airborne. Symptoms include a runny nose, severe cough, and a pause between breaths (apnea). Complications include pneumonia and death.

The flu vaccine protects your child from *influenza,* which is airborne and contracted through direct contact. Symptoms include muscle pain, cough, fatigue, sore throat, and fever. Complications can lead to pneumonia.

If you're traveling, please speak to your doctor about any additional vaccines your baby may need.

Side Effects of Vaccines and How to Manage Them

Common side effects include fever, a small lump at the injection site, tenderness, swelling, and redness around the site, a restless baby, or an oddly drowsy baby.

Here's some advice on how to treat these side effects:

- You may use a cold, wet towel for compression twice a day to help a site lump go down faster. However, it should go down on its own.
- Change your baby's clothes when they're hot so you don't encourage a fever.
- Allow your baby some extra fluids to rehydrate.
- You can speak to your doctor about liquid form paracetamol for your baby to ease the pain and bring their fever down. Just remember that your baby needs natural probiotics whenever they're taking any form of medication. A smooth, plain spoonful of yogurt before each intake of medication helps your baby's tummy deal with medications.

There are some rare side effects of vaccinations, too. One of the rare side effects is anaphylaxis, which should be treated by your doctor or emergency staff. It's a severe allergic reaction to the vaccination, and is completely treatable if handled swiftly. Another rare side effect is a blockage of their bowels. This is highly unlikely to happen if you keep your baby hydrated. Finally, a one or two-minute febrile seizure can take place, which scares the hair off your head. Febrile seizures happen when a child's temperature rises too fast (Immunisation – Side Effects, 2018). However, your doctor will bring your baby's fever down quickly.

Weighing the Risks and Benefits

Refusing your baby's vaccinations can place your baby, your family, and everyone around you at risk for serious complications and diseases. Vaccinations are medication that help you prevent serious illness or even death for your baby. Any side effects are easily manageable, and serious side effects are rare. The benefits outweigh the risks. If you have followed the guidelines in this book and have your doctor close by, you have nothing to worry about (Immunisation – Side Effects, 2018).

I apologise for the brutal information in this section, but you need to learn the hard facts about vaccinations. Now you can take a deep breath and relax as we move onto the next chapter.

Chapter 12: Baby's Safety and Medical Emergency Concerns

A crucial part of raising a healthy baby is to ensure their safety, and to know when to call for help. In this chapter, we'll look at important safety measures, emergency situations, and travel tips.

Home and Outdoor Safety

The Nursery

There are a few ways to make your nursery safer for your explorative little one. Let's delve into the details (St Clair DiLaura, n.d).

Anchor your furniture: Your baby is a strong and curious soul who loves to explore. Make sure that all nursery furniture is anchored against the wall or floor, secured with studs or drywall screws. You want your baby to be able to pull themselves up against furniture when they start learning to lift themselves — secure furniture isn't only safe, but it gives your baby the freedom of learning to stand.

Toy storage: Yes, your baby is going to have a mountain of toys. You should ensure that your toy chest has no sharp edges and that any lid can be easily removed. You don't want your baby trapped in the toy chest or injured by a falling lid. I had a special toy chest made for my kids. It was made of thick, durable plastic that had rounded edges, and instead of inserting the toys at the top, it was open in the front. Sure, it was larger than other "toy chests," and messier — but it was safer, too.

Declutter the nursery: You should remove all small items from your baby's reach. Pack everything in drawers and make sure the drawers are locked. This includes any choking hazards, disposable diapers, creams, ointments, toiletries, coins, anything small enough to fit in their mouth, and anything long enough to string around their neck or hands. You'll be surprised what your baby will want to shove in their mouth or bite; it's the way they learn.

Electricity: Your baby is curious as heck and wants to touch everything and place everything in their ear, nose, and mouth. I had a shelf that was high up on the wall and placed everything there after each use. And don't forget the outlets. You can purchase fake covers for each outlet in your house. It looks like a flat plug that you insert so that your baby can't stick their wet little fingers into an outlet.

Secure your windows: If you have blinds in your nursery, remove any decorative strings attached to them, and when you open or close them, make sure to secure the strings up high again. Additionally, your baby is going to climb out of curiosity. Remove any furniture that can help your baby get near the window.

Crib: Issue number one with cribs is safety standards. Yes, I know, cribs are pricey, but you should avoid your ancestral crib. Safety standards for cribs have changed and improvements have been made. The old drop-side models were painted with lead paint and their slats are too far apart.

Furthermore, the AAP advises against the use of crib bumpers and too many loose, soft items around your baby. Remove any extra blankets, duvets, pillows, and teddy bears from your baby's crib. You should also place your crib away from the wall and avoid hanging a mobile overhead. As your baby gets stronger and uses their surroundings to lift themselves, they'll pull anything down. You can hang pictures against the wall if you use earthquake-safe screws and your crib is away from the wall. Mobiles look cute, but they're a dangling hazard.

Feeding Safety

Food safety is another important aspect. I've compiled some advice on food safety that hasn't been mentioned yet, but if your baby was premature, had a low birth weight, or your baby's unhealthy, you need to speak to your pediatrician about this topic (NSW Food Authority, 2015).

When it comes to breastfeeding, make sure you follow the guidelines I provided earlier to store your milk properly, and keep your hands sanitized at all times. Formula should be prepared with sterilized hands, too. Wash your hands with warm water and antibacterial soap, and you should do the same with any countertops you use for preparation.

You should avoid using homemade formula, because this isn't restricted or regulated by FDA guidelines. Homemade formula often uses raw milk or raw milk products and contains several disease-causing organisms.

As far as solid foods go, you must avoid raw or partially-cooked eggs because they could contain salmonella. Eggs need to be hard-boiled and then mashed for your baby's consumption. Honey can't be fed to babies younger than 12 months, as this can cause botulism. Finally, salt can harm your baby's kidneys, because their kidneys are still developing and cannot expel the excess salt. Besides, your baby's taste buds are still developing, too, and they don't need to grow accustomed to salt and spices.

Every single utensil, cup, bottle, and nipple your baby eats with needs to be rinsed in cold water, washed in warm, antibacterial soapy water with a bottle brush, and then rinsed again before you sterilize them using steam or hot water. Fortunately, there are modern-day steamers for baby bottles which come with easy-to-follow instructions. Otherwise, you can boil all these eating utensils in a pot of water for two minutes and add a sterilizing agent purchased from your local drug store. Remember not to use excessive heat.

The Bathroom

Next, I'll focus on some bathroom safety tips (The Editors of Parents Magazine, n.d).

You can start securing your bathroom by removing any hazardous items. These can include razors, hair clips, toothbrushes, make-up, and soap. Fasten a shelf against the wall, out of reach of your baby, and place all these hazardous items on the shelf. Make sure they can't fall off the shelf by labeling some containers and placing all loose items inside. Remember that your baby will eat your soap. You can also secure your laundry basket against the wall so they don't crawl into it or topple it over on themselves, and do the same with the garbage bin. Finally, you should throw out any cat litter box, because your child will eat it. Your kitty will have to use their litter box outside.

Watch out for any water hazards. Get into the habit of running your water out after each bath, no matter how little water was used. You should secure all water outlets with padded child-proof knobs to prevent your baby from burning against the hot surface and opening the faucet. You should also check that your water heater isn't set above 120 degrees.

Next, you need to check all electrical outlets again and cover them once more. Hair dryers and electric shavers should be stored out of reach after every use. Hide all cords and wires that can wrap around any part of your baby or that your baby can chew on.

Your medicine cabinet needs a change, too. Yes, it's convenient to keep your medication in the bathroom, but you need to either place a lock on the cabinet or move it away from the basin and fasten it securely to a wall that has no climbing assistance underneath. The same goes for any cleaning chemicals or toiletries. These should all be placed in a child-proof, locked cabinet.

Finally, throw out your old bathroom rugs and replace them with rubberized non-slip rugs to secure your baby's first wobbly steps. You can use a rubber mat in the bathtub as well for when they start bathing in the tub.

The Front Garden and Backyard

The garden is another place many people forget to secure properly, but your baby will spend time there and it should be as safe as possible (How to Make Every Yard Safe, n.d).

Your garden can be a treacherous arena for your baby, and it's important to look at your groundcover and hazards. Start by removing all plant fertilizers and tools by placing them in a locked shed. Then you can look around your garden and remove any garden terrifying gnomes, sharp garden bed surroundings, and rocks. If they're fixed in the ground, dig them up and toss them.

Next, if you have a pool, make sure it's securely fenced in and there's no way for your baby to access it. You can also fence your wood pile, barbecue, and anything that doesn't go into your garden shed. Do away with any glass-top tables and metal outdoor chairs.

Finally, if you have a playground, make sure your swing or slide is surrounded by soft, shock-absorbing ground cover like grass or rubber mats. Avoid rope swings and use chain swings, instead. Additionally, make sure your slide ends where there's no hazards around and keep a sand pit covered from pets and bugs that will contaminate it.

General Safety Tips

Here are a few more safety tips to consider when your baby is around the house (Safety Inside and Outside the House, 2019).

You can prevent burns by keeping hot things out of reach, turning pot handles away from the edge of the counter, never allowing electrical cords like a kettle cord to hang within reach, using a fire guard around your fireplace and radiator, and removing tablecloths. In addition, keep lighters, matches, and Christmas tree lights away from your baby.

To prevent falls, you can round furniture corners or add pads to them, avoid allowing your baby to sleep on a bed instead of their crib, use the seatbelt in your highchair, and teach your baby to stop climbing up onto high things. Furthermore, you shouldn't leave your baby unattended on a high surface and install baby barriers or keep doors locked to keep them away from dangerous areas.

Sadly, as little as a few teaspoons of water can harm your baby, which is why you need to remove any pools of water that gather after some rain, never leave your baby unattended in water, and drain the baby splash pool when you're done.

Furthermore, you should avoid buying toys that aren't age appropriate. Your baby's toys should be checked regularly for splinters, sharp edges, and loose bits. You should buy soft or large toys with no small breakable parts. Keep safe toys low so your baby doesn't need to climb to reach it, and avoid walkers altogether. I know that sounds crazy but walkers have all those little buttons on the front that tend to break off and become a choking hazard.

Remember that your baby knows nothing and they need to be taught. Your baby will fall and bump their little noggin here and there; it's all part of learning. There's no need to panic — just remain vigilant and supervise your baby at all times. If you've taken all the necessary precautions, you can take a breath of relief because you've minimized the chances of accidents.

Unwell Baby: When to Seek Help

Let's face it, your baby will have a fever or vomit from time to time. I'll cover common reasons for seeking medical attention from your pediatrician in this section, because whether you're a new parent or a first-time parent, it remains challenging to identify an unwell baby. Here are some signs that your baby needs medical attention that haven't been covered yet in this book (Mayo Clinic Staff, 2019):

Fever: Your baby has a concerning fever if they are younger than three months; your three- to six-month-old baby's temperature is 102 degrees or higher and accompanied by other symptoms; your six-month-old baby's fever is above 102 with other symptoms; or there are no other symptoms and their fever persists for more than a day.

Tender navel or penis: Contact your pediatrician if your baby's navel or penis turns red and starts to bleed.

Dehydration: Additional signs of severe dehydration include a sunken soft spot on their head, dry mouth, and no tears when they cry.

Changes in appetite: Your baby's eating too little or has refused food for the last few feedings.

Changes in behavior: Your baby may cry more than usual, be more floppy, sleep more than they normally do, or they don't allow you to comfort their cries.

The common cold: It becomes worrisome when your baby's nasal mucus lasts longer than 10 to 14 days, they have trouble breathing, or they suffer from a cough or ear pain for more than a week.

Eye discharge: Watch out for red eyes that leak any form of mucus.

When to Seek Emergency Care

Before an incident happens, you can ask your doctor for advice on how to treat certain symptoms on your way to the hospital. After my own scare that Saturday night, I took a first aid course that specializes in babies. I paid $88 for it at the time, and I don't regret it one bit. It helped me cope with a few emergencies over the years while I was en route to the hospital. However, you should seek emergency care for any of the following signs or symptoms, because I'm not a licensed healthcare provider (Mayo Clinic Staff, 2019).

- Your baby's choking.
- They got burned with boiling water or against a hot surface.
- Your baby's having a seizure. They'll become less responsive and they may foam from their mouth.
- You can't stop their bleeding.

- They suffered an electrical shock from a power outlet or cord.
- Your baby's skin and face turned blue, purple, or grey.
- An animal or person bit them.
- They had a near-drowning incident in any amount of water.
- They suffered an injury to their head or face after a fall.
- If their skin or eye came into contact with any poisonous substance.
- If they inhaled a poisonous substance.
- If they accidentally consumed a poisonous substance.
- If their breathing is labored or they've stopped breathing. Your baby will need cardiopulmonary resuscitation (CPR). This is one of the first things they teach you with first aid, and I suggest you take a class.

However, it's important to know why your baby's in the condition they're in. The medical staff can help your baby faster if you know what happened. These are questions they may ask you upon arrival at the emergency room.

1. What symptoms does your baby have?
2. What's your baby's medical history? (Having their history at hand is a great idea. Make sure it's always ready in the car.)
3. Has your baby had any changes in their feeding, bowel movements, or temperature?
4. Have you tried any home remedies we need to be aware of?
5. What possible toxins, environmental factors, foods, or dangerous elements has your baby been exposed to?

Keep in mind that when your baby needs urgent care, the best thing you can do is keep a clear head and do what needs to be done. Standing in a corner and freaking out won't help your baby. Allow your autopilot to take over and steer yourself to a solution.

Traveling With an Infant

Finally, I'd like to cover travel tips for you and your baby. Having a baby doesn't mean you don't have to travel, you should just be better prepared before you do (Wears, 2013).

If you're planning to fly, there are a few things to consider. Call the airline and check whether the flight is fully booked. If it isn't, ask them to block off the middle seat and book the aisle and window seat. You'll want some space for supplies and your partner can have the aisle seat opposite you. You'll also need your car seat, and you should make sure it's up to standard with flying regulations — not all of them are. Don't forget to let the airline know that you'll be traveling with your baby.

Pack well for a flight, because airlines charge for extra luggage — and your stroller and car seat are considered extra luggage. Take into consideration your hand luggage, too, because you'll need baby essentials more than your make-up bag. Another item I packed was extra cotton wool. Flights can make babies' ears hurt and you can use cotton wool soaked in warm water to insert into their ears to help. Besides the essentials, you'll need entertainment for your baby to distract them from boredom and crying, so pack a toy or two in your hand luggage that you can use to play with your baby.

If you're traveling abroad, pack your formula, breast pump, and baby foods into your luggage. Just remember to include these food items on your declaration checklist. Chances are, they won't have the formula or food your baby loves and you'll have trouble feeding them. Next, you can pack the stroller that suits your trip. If you're stopping multiple times on your journey, pack a light, easily foldable stroller. However, if you're doing a lot of sightseeing when you get there, you may need a stronger stroller in which your baby can nap. Furthermore, a car seat is required by law in most countries, so don't forget your car seat even if your cruising over on a ship.

Call your hotel before you confirm your booking and tell them about your baby. You can request a room that's away from others so your baby won't cry people awake, and you can ask them if their rooms are baby-friendly with cribs.

Finally, make sure you plan ahead for your baby's vaccinations. They may need additional shots, depending on your destination. Do your homework and ensure a memorable holiday for all of you.

Conclusion

Congratulations, you've made it — and don't you simply feel relieved now? Before you started this book, you were in a state of confusion and doubt. You struggled to believe in yourself and your ability to bring a beautiful, healthy baby into this world and raise them for the first 12 months. You were overwhelmed by worries about pregnancy and all it entails. Even if this is your second baby, you weren't sure about your previous knowledge and methodology. You never expected to feel those underlying concerns a second or third time around, yet, they were present. If you're new to being a parent, you saw parenthood as an insurmountable task ahead of you. You didn't believe that you had it in you to overcome that terrifyingly big obstacle.

You found yourself staring up at a giant, barely able to catch your breath. You could feel your feet slipping over the edge of pre- and postnatal sanity. You weren't sure how you would carry another human being inside of you. You questioned how your body could handle two people at once. You found yourself worrying about your health during pregnancy, and the health of your baby before and after pregnancy. Suddenly, your mind was flooded with ideas about what to do after your baby was born. You felt weak and uneducated, whether you'd been a parent before or not, whether you're an expectant mother or father.

However, after finishing this book, you feel a strong sense of freedom from these horrid concerns, and you know you're ready for whatever pregnancy and the first year of your baby's life can throw your way. Among many topics, we've covered essential know-how in this book, including:

- Choosing the right doctor or midwife for your pregnancy;
- An in-depth look at your prenatal check-ups;
- All the medication, supplements, and the

best diet for your pregnancy journey;
- The impact of your possible smoking, caffeine, and alcoholic habits;
- Finding rest and preparing for the big day;
- Realistic expectations of the first 24 hours and the 12 months that follow;
- Postnatal care and essential check-ups;
- What to do and what not to do;
- Immunizations and how they impact your baby;
- Recovering from the birth of your baby;
- The need-to-know basics of your baby's skincare, health, hygiene, and nutrition;
- Concerns about baby illnesses and red flag alerts;
- Securing your baby's environment to keep them safe.

I know how challenging motherhood or fatherhood can be, and that's why this book covers all the topics I know concerned me. There are typical questions all parents-to-be will want answered, and I've provided straightforward knowledge and experience to correctly portray solutions. You might find yourself doubting something your mother told you. Here, I've used information from reliable and modern sources to back my own experience and knowledge. There are things I learned while writing this book that helped me understand the reason why my baby had those vaccinations. The average Joe doesn't know the scientific reasons behind them and will think it's okay to skip one.

I've come across information on pregnancy that I didn't know and other data that I did. I can guarantee you that the knowledge shared in this book helped you heal your C-section wound, reminded you of every item you needed on the first day, prevented harm from befalling your baby, taught you how to hold your baby correctly when breastfeeding, and explained useful methods to bond with your baby. Additionally, it helped you overcome concerns about what you'll do when your baby falls ill after hours, what foods to avoid while pregnant, what foods to avoid giving your baby, and how to distinguish one skin condition from another.

Furthermore, you've learned about what's normal in your baby's urine, birthmarks, common ailments, and when to call your pediatrician. We've covered questions and answers that needed to be asked, which helped you choose your doctor. You found comfort in knowing that you can hold your baby a certain way, you can use certain methods to help them sleep, and you've even prepared for childcare if you do go back to work or just need a night off. Your brain has soaked up enough information to give you the best chance of providing the greatest future to your baby.

Here comes the most difficult part. This book is filled with information that can only allow you to take a step forward. However, if there's one thing I want you to take away from this book, it's that you need to ask for help when you're unsure about anything. There's absolutely no shame in seeking assistance from a friend, a family member, your partner, or even a support group you may be part of. I could never imagine having completed my pregnancy journey, or the first year, if my loving partner hadn't been by my side.

If you choose to delve deeper into any concerns you may have, make sure you confirm your findings. Google is a wonderful tool, but anything you find online should be checked with your supportive partner, evidence-based facts, or other people you confide in. So go out there and gather up your support group, keep this book close by for reference, and take the bull by its horns.

References

10 Reasons to Get Vaccinated (n.d) Retrieved from www.nfid.org/immunization/10-reasons-to-get-vaccinated/

11 Ways to Handle New Baby Stress. (January 11, 2018) Retrieved from https://blog.pregakem.com/handle-new-baby-stress.html

Alli, R.A. (February 25, 2019) Get the Facts About Bottle Feeding. Retrieved from www.webmd.com/parenting/baby/ss/slideshow-baby-bottles

American College of Obstetricians and Gynecologists (June 2019) Travel During Pregnancy. Retrieved from www.acog.org/Patients/FAQs/Travel-During-Pregnancy?IsMobileSet=falseWorking

American Pregnancy Association (2019) Diet During Pregnancy. Retrieved from https://americanpregnancy.org/pregnancy-health/diet-during-pregnancy/

American Pregnancy Association (2019) Eating Seafood During Pregnancy. Retrieved from https://americanpregnancy.org/pregnancy-health/eating-seafood-during-pregnancy/

American Pregnancy Association (2019) Getting Sick While Pregnant. Retrieved from https://americanpregnancy.org/pregnancy-complications/sick-while-pregnant/

American Pregnancy Association (2019) Natural Sources of Vitamin B6 During Pregnancy. Retrieved from https://americanpregnancy.org/pregnancy-health/natural-sources-of-vitamin-b6-during-pregnancy/

American Pregnancy Association (2019) Pregnancy Nutrition. Retrieved from https://americanpregnancy.org/pregnancy-health/pregnancy-nutrition/

American Pregnancy Association (2019) Types of Prenatal Vitamins. Retrieved from https://americanpregnancy.org/pregnancy-health/types-prenatal-vitamins/

American Pregnancy Association (2019) Vitamin D and Pregnancy. Retrieved from https://americanpregnancy.org/pregnancy-health/vitamin-d-and-pregnancy/

Apgar Score (October, 2017) Retrieved from www.pregnancybirthbaby.org.au/apgar-score

Arora, M. (August 16, 2019) Bottle Feeding Advantages and Disadvantages. Retrieved from https://parenting.firstcry.com/articles/bottle-feeding-advantages-and-disadvantages/

Avery, N. (2018) 10 Tips for Coping with a New Baby. Retrieved from https://planningwithkids.com/2009/05/12/10-tips-for-coping-with-a-new-baby/

Baby's First 24 Hours (June, 2018) Retrieved from www.pregnancybirthbaby.org.au/babys-first-24-hours

Bell, K. (2009) Diaper Duty Essentials: What's Normal? Retrieved from www.parents.com/baby/diapers/dirty/diaper-duty-essentials-whats-normal/

Bloch, E. (n.d) Are Generic Formulas as Good as Brand Names? Retrieved from www.parents.com/baby/feeding/are-generic-formulas-as-good-as-name-brands/

Boyd-Barret, C. & Alrahmani, L. (October 28, 2019) C-section healing and recovery time. Retrieved from www.babycenter.com/0_recovering-from-a-c-section_221.bc

Breastfeeding at Work (n.d) Retrieved from www.ameda.com/milk-101-article/breastfeeding-at-work/

Breastfeeding Overview (2019) P. 1–5. Retrieved from www.webmd.com/parenting/baby/nursing-basics#1-2

Breast Pumping Guide: When and How Long to Pump (n.d) Retrieved from www.ameda.com/milk-101-article/when-and-how-long-to-pump/

Breastmilk Storage Guidelines: How to Store Milk Safely (n.d) Retrieved from www.ameda.com/milk-101-article/how-to-store-breast-milk-safely/

Carepoint Health (February 17, 2015) Surviving pregnancy without your favorite vices. Retrieved from https://carepointhealth.org/surviving-pregnancy-without-favorite-vices/

Centers for Disease Control and Prevention (February 5, 2019) 2019 Recommended Vaccinations for Infants and Children (birth through 6 years) Parent-Friendly Format. Retrieved from www.cdc.gov/vaccines/schedules/easy-to-read/child-easyread.html#table-child

Check-ups, tests and scans available during your pregnancy (2018) Retrieved from www.pregnancybirthbaby.org.au/checkups-and-scans-during-your-pregnancy

Childbirth Connection (2016) What to Ask a Midwife Who Might Provide Your Maternity Care. Retrieved from www.nationalpartnership.org/research-library/maternal-health/what-to-ask-midwife.pdf

Childbirth Connection (2016) What to Ask a Physician Who May Provide Your Maternity Care. Retrieved from www.nationalpartnership.org/research-library/maternal-health/what-to-ask-physician.pdf

Childbirth Connection (n.d) Retrieved from www.childbirthconnection.org/healthy-pregnancy/choosing-a-care-provider/collecting-information/

Cleveland Clinic (September 24, 2018) Pregnancy Bed Rest. Retrieved from https://my.clevelandclinic.org/health/articles/9757-pregnancy-bed-rest

DeStefano, F.; Price, C.S.; & Weintraub, E.S. (2013) The Journal of Pediatrics. P. 561. Increasing Exposure to Antibody-Stimulating Proteins and Polysaccharides in Vaccines is Not Associated with Risk of Autism. Retrieved from www.jpeds.com/article/S0022-3476(13)00144-3/pdf?ext=.pdf

Ding, K. (2019) Sleep Deprivation and New Parents. Retrieved from https://consumer.healthday.com/encyclopedia/parenting-31/parenting-health-news-525/sleep-deprivation-and-new-parents-643886.html

Dorning, A. (March 20, 2019) Childcare Options: Pros, Cons, and Costs. Retrieved from www.babycenter.com/childcare-options

Flaxman, S.M. & Sherman, P.W. (June, 2000) The Quarterly Review of Biology. Vol. 75, No. 2, P. 113-148

Fritz, A. (October 14, 2019) The Best Maternity Underwear to Keep You Comfortable Throughout Your Pregnancy. Retrieved from www.whattoexpect.com/baby-products/pregnancy/maternity-underwear/

Hodnett, E.D. (2002) Pain and women's satisfaction with the experience of childbirth: a systematic review. Retrieved from www.ncbi.nih.gov/m/pubmed/12011880/#

How to Make Every Yard Safe (n.d) Retrieved from www.safetyed.org/howtomakeeveryyardsafe.html#.XeYP70BuLIV?

How Vaccines Work (2019) Retrieved from www.publichealth.org/public-awareness/understanding-vaccines/vaccines-work/

Introducing Solid Foods to Your Baby (June 11, 2019) Retrieved from www.healthlinkbc.ca/health-topics/te4473

Immunisation Side Effects (April, 2018) Retrieved from www.betterhealth.vic.gov.au/health/healthyliving/immunisation-side-effects

Johnson, T.C. (May 16, 2018) Pregnancy Fitness: Your Best Moves Before Baby Arrives. Retrieved from www.webmd.com/baby/ss/slideshow-pregnancy-fitness-moves

Khan, A. (June 20, 2018) Washing Your Baby's Clothes – How to do it Rightly. Retrieved from https://parenting.firstcry.com/articles/washing-your-babys-clothes-how-to-do-it-rightly/

Khan, A. (May 22, 2018) 21 Common Pregnancy Problems and Their Solutions. Retrieved from https://parenting.firstcry.com/articles/21-common-pregnancy-problems-and-their-solutions/

Klein, M. (1993) The effectiveness of family practice maternity care. Primary Care, Iss 20 (3), P. 523–536.

Louie, K. (August 20, 2018) Best Pregnancy-Safe Makeup and Beauty Products. Retrieved from www.whattoexpect.com/maternity-products/beauty/best-pregnancy-safe-makeup/

Marcin, A. & Westphalen, D. (September 14, 2018) What Medicines Can I Take While Pregnant? Retrieved from www.healthline.com/health/pregnancy/what-medicines-are-safe-during-pregnancy

Maternity Leave in the United States (November 26, 2019) Retrieved from https://en.wikipedia.org/wiki/Maternity_leave_in_the_United_States#Current_legislation

Mayo Clinic Staff (August 13, 2019) Sick Baby? When to Seek Medical Attention. Retrieved from www.mayoclinic.org/healthy-lifestyle/infant-and-toddler-health/in-depth/healthy-baby/art-20047793

Mayo Clinic Staff (February 17, 2018) Umbilical Cord Care: Do's and Don'ts for Parents. Retrieved from www.mayoclinic.org/healthy-lifestyle/infant-and-toddler-health/in-depth/umbilical-cord/art-20048250

Mayo Clinic Staff (June 6, 2019) Solid foods: How to get your baby started. Retrieved from www.mayoclinic.org/healthy-lifestyle/infant-and-toddler-health/in-depth/healthy-baby/art-20046200

Miller, K. (January 31, 2019) 7 Ways to Make Sleep More Comfortable When You're Pregnant. Retrieved from www.self.com/story/pregnancy-sleep-comfort

Montgomery, N. (January 9, 2019) How to Trim Your Baby's Nails. Retrieved from www.babycenter.com/0_how-to-trim-your-babys-nails_10027.bc

Murkoff, H. & The What to Expect Editors (December 19, 2018) Newborn Circumcision Care. Retrieved from www.whattoexpect.com/first-year/circumcision-care

Murkoff, H. & The What to Expect Editors (January 9, 2019) Essentials for Diaper Changing Stations. Retrieved from www.whattoexpect.com/baby-products/diapering-potty/essentials-for-diaper-changing-stations/

Murkoff, H. & The What to Expect Editors (March 30, 2019) Baby's First Bath. Retrieved from www.whattoexpect.com/first-year/first-bath/

Murkoff, H. & The What to Expect Editors (November 27, 2018) 5 Strategies for Working While Pregnant. Retrieved from www.whattoexpect.com/pregnancy/working-while-pregnant

Nagin, M.K. & Shur, M. (November 13, 2019) Self-Care for the Breastfeeding Mother. Retrieved from www.verywellfamily.com/taking-care-of-the-breastfeeding-mother-431683

Newborn Rashes and Skin Conditions (December 12, 2018) Retrieved from www.uofmhealth.org/health-library/zx1747

Nishapro (May 4, 2018) Shopping Tips for Newborn Baby's Clothes. Retrieved from https://community.today.com/parentingteam/post/shopping-tips-for-newborn-babys-clothes

NSW Food Authority (March, 2015) Retrieved from www.sahealth.sa.gov.au/wps/wcm/connect/5514158047d940a7ac79adfc651ee2b2/Feeding+babies+and+food+safety+Fact+Sheet.pdf?MOD=AJPERES

Pillai, S. (November 8, 2019) 5 Reasons Why it is Unsafe to Have Deli Meats in Pregnancy. Retrieved from www.momjunction.com/articles/is-it-safe-to-eat-deli-meats-during-pregnancy_00118527/#gref

Recovery After Vaginal Birth (August, 2017) Retrieved from www.babycentre.co.uk/a553491/recovery-after-vaginal-birth

Reutter, K. (November 16, 2018) 8 Ways to Treat Morning Sickness Naturally. Retrieved from www.onemedical.com/blog/get-well/natural-morning-sickness-remedies

Rhesus D Negative in Pregnancy (May, 2018) Retrieved from www.pregnancybirthbaby.org.au/rhesus-d-negative-in-pregnancy

Safety Inside and Outside the House (September 24, 2019) Retrieved from www.facs.nsw.gov.au/families/parenting/keeping-children-safe/around-the-house/chapters/at-home

Schmitt, J.W. (April 1, 2019) Prenatal Care. Retrieved from www.womenshealth.gov/a-z-topics/prenatal-care

Sheahan, K.P. (September, 2019) Choosing a Pediatrician for Your New Baby. Retrieved from https://kidshealth.org/en/parents/find-ped.html

Shortsleeve, C. (June 10, 2019) The Best Maternity Jeans for Every Body Type. Retrieved from www.whattoexpect.com/baby-products/maternity/best-maternity-jeans/

SickKids Staff (January 7, 2019) Health Issues in Your Newborn Baby. Retrieved from www.aboutkidshealth.ca/Article?contentid=453&language=English

St Clair DiLaura, A. (n.d) Creating a Safe Nursery: 10 Mistakes to Avoid. Retrieved from www.babycenter.com/101_creating-a-safe-nursery-10-mistakes-to-avoid_10414382.bc

Tellado, M.P. (September, 2019) Diaper Rash. Retrieved from https://kidshealth.org/en/parents/diaper-rash.html

The Editors of Parents Magazine (n.d) 5 Things You Can Do to Get a Safer Bathroom. Retrieved from www.parents.com/baby/safety/bathroom/bathroom-safety-basics/

The Ultimate Maternity Hospital Bag Checklist (May 1, 2019) Retrieved from www.pampers.com/en-us/pregnancy/giving-birth/article/what-to-pack-in-your-hospital-bag-go-bag-checklist

UPMC Magee-Women's Hospital (March 23, 2016) How Smoking, Alcohol, and Drugs Can Harm Your Baby. Retrieved from https://share.upmc.com/2016/03/how-smoking-alcohol-drugs-harm-your-baby/

Vaccine Safety (October 22, 2018) Retrieved from www.cdc.gov/vaccinesafety/concerns/adjuvants.html

Vitamin K at Birth (June, 2018) www.pregnancybirthbaby.org.au/vitamin-k-at-birth

Weaning Your Child from Breastfeeding (June, 2019) Retrieved from www.caringforkids.cps.ca/handouts/weaning_breastfeeding

Wears, C. (September 2, 2013) Traveling with an Infant: 8 Things You Must Know Before You Go. Retrieved from www.flightnetwork.com/blog/traveling-with-an-infant-things-to-know-before-you-go/

What a Newborn Looks Like (August, 2017) Retrieved from www.babycentre.co.uk/a178/what-a-newborn-looks-like

What is Newborn Screening? (November 26, 2019) Retrieved from https://ghr.nlm.nih.gov/primer/newbornscreening/nbs

What to Expect Editors (May 21, 2019) Prenatal Appointments. www.whattoexpect.com/pregnancy/pregnancy-health/prenatal-appointments/

Yang, S. (2019) Baby's Check-Up Schedule. Retrieved from www.thebump.com/a/new-baby-doctor-visit-checklist